Private Client Practice:
An Expert Guide
2nd edition

EDITED BY LAURA SLATER

Head of legal publishing
Fiona Fleming

Publisher
Helen Donegan

Editor
Laura Slater

Published by
Globe Law and Business Ltd
3 Mylor Close
Horsell
Woking
Surrey GU21 4DD
United Kingdom
Tel: +44 20 3745 4770
www.globelawandbusiness.com

ISBN: 978-1-78358-227-3
A catalogue record for this book is available from the British Library

Contents

Executive summary

The past year has brought a swathe of significant changes affecting the core areas of private client work, including tax, pensions, estates, and trusts. With private client matters often straddling practice areas and increasingly stretching across borders, keeping on top of the developments that might affect clients is becoming an increasingly tall order for all those who work in this area. The second edition of *Private Client Practice: An Expert Guide* shares expert insight into the key changes affecting this busy sector, helping practitioners to offer the most up-to-date, pertinent advice to their clients.

Broken into a series of direct and insightful articles from a broad range of legal and financial experts in the private client sphere, the guide outlines the most important legislative and case law developments and considers their practical impact. Articles also address some of some tricky and related areas that private client solicitors should know about, such as investment strategies, farming law, and litigation.

While private client practitioners are no strangers to change, many of the developments of the past year have sent vibrations throughout the sector. Accordingly, the opening article in this guide provides a broad overview of the most important changes of the past 12 months. These topics are then picked up and built upon throughout the book.

The UK tax landscape, in particular, has undergone a revolution in the past year, especially in the wake of the Summer Budget 2015. As part of the round-up of the latest changes and developments affecting private client work, the next chapter weighs up the potential 'winners' and 'losers' of the recent inheritance tax changes.

This is followed by an article which takes a closer look at one group of potential 'losers' in the shake up: non-domiciliaries. In a climate where 'non-doms' have become an easy target for political point scoring, this chapter outlines the particular challenges of advising these clients on their tax status, and explains why it is essential to keep ahead of the curve in this frequently changing sector.

Clean capital is a central component of UK tax planning for non-doms and this is the focus of the next article in this book. Martyn Wildney and Mark Davies of Mark Davies & Associates provide insight into the opportunities, benefits, and pitfalls for clients looking to ring-fence their foreign assets and earnings from UK taxation through clean capital.

Continuing the theme of advising clients on their international assets – a situation which is going to be increasingly common as migration continues to grow – the next contributor discusses the challenges of planning a worldwide estate, commenting on the new EU succession laws, and variations and conflicts in law between countries.

This is followed by a focus on farmland succession, which – with an aging farming population and as the value of farmland increases – is also a growing area of challenging work for private client solicitors. Farm tax expert Julie Butler outlines recent changes in England and Wales and Scotland that those working with farming clients should be aware of.

One of the highest profile cases of 2015 was that of *Ilott v Mitson*; the decision in the most recent of five court decisions, in July of 2015, has potentially significant implications for testators and their beneficiaries. The next contributor asks what are the practical implications of the *Ilott* decsion, taking the question both from the point of view of the non-litigator drawing up a will to avoid 1975 Act challenges, and that of the litigator who may be asked to fight a claim.

Also amongst the possible 'losers' of recent government legislation are individuals looking to safeguard their assets for future generations by settling them in trusts. While the recent reforms have made trusts a less attractive proposition than they once were, as the next contributors to this guide explain, there are still many circumstances where they may still be justifiable and highly beneficial – the important thing is to keep your client's principal motivation in mind.

The possibility of passing pension savings down generations is one of the many potential benefits of the new 'pension freedoms' introduced in 2015, according to Penny Cogher, pensions partner at Irwin Mitchell. The next article in this guide considers this and other opportunities and pitfalls of the April 2015 pension reforms – much discussed by press and public – and asks what they really mean for individuals and practitioners.

For many clients, planning for the future also means preparing for the possibility of future care fees. The Care Act 2014 partially came into force on 1 April 2015, but the issue of who pays for care continues to be a contentious topic. With the second phase of provisions now controversially postponed until 2020, the next article in this book, from continuing healthcare expert Lisa Morgan of Hugh James LLP, looks back at how far we have come since this landmark piece of legislation was introduced and considers the likely future of paying for care.

Active or passive? That is the question when it comes to asset management and the answer is never straightforward. In the next article in this book, Claire Bennison, regional director of Brooks MacDonald Asset Management, assesses the relative merits of active and passive investment strategies, and considers where the two can be combined.

The variety of contributors to this guide is illustrative of the breadth of private client practice. More so than in many other practice areas, private client solicitors have to be able to think outside the silo when considering how to provide individual clients with a service that meets their needs – even if that means referring clients to colleagues in other practice areas, or possibly professional contacts outside the firm, for complementary advice. This book concludes, appropriately, with an article in which SIFA chairman Ian Muirhead discusses how legal and financial advisors can work better together to ensure their clients receive the best, most rounded advice possible.

Private client practitioners provide a variety of services at the heart of which is an individual in need of advice; providing a client-centric service should be the aim of all those who work in this area. The chapters in this guide share a wide range of expertise and experience designed to help practitioners to achieve that aim.

About the authors

Claire Bennison joined Brooks Macdonald in 2007 as regional director. Claire has over 26 years of investment and management experience. Her most recent role, prior to joining Brooks Macdonald, was as a director of Barclays Wealth, where she was head of technical analysis and currencies and a member of the Asset Allocation Committee, formulating investment strategy across all asset classes and regions for private clients. She has continued to bring this experience to Brooks Macdonald, focusing on both structural and tactical asset allocation as well as looking at developing investment solutions reflecting clients' specific requirements and circumstances.

Claire is a member of the Brooks Macdonald Asset Allocation Committee and sits on the Brooks Macdonald Asset Management Board. She heads up the three regional offices in the North of England and is responsible for the future development of the region and the teams. Claire has a Master of Business Administration from the University of Liverpool and is a chartered fellow of the Chartered Institute for Securities & Investments (CISI).

Julie Butler FCA founded the firm of Butler & Co in 1986 and currently has two offices in Hampshire with a dedicated and experienced team. She has built up an extensive knowledge of tax issues affecting high net worth individuals, including farmers, landowners, and those involved in equestrian activities, and she has also recently passed her ICAEW probate exam. Her articles are published in the national accountancy and tax press and she is the author of *Tax Planning for Farm and Land Diversification and Equine Tax Planning*, as well as co-author of *Stanley: Taxation of Farmers and Landowners* with Malcolm Gunn.

Julie and her team carry out a large amount of consultancy work for other accountants and solicitors on farming diversification and bloodstock in areas of tax planning and complex tax enquiries. Julie writes regularly in all the technical tax press and has a reputation for a fresh approach to subjects such as wind farms, bio-fuels, woodlands, furnished holiday lets, and all farm property concerns in this current complicated economic climate. Julie lectures regularly to a large variety of audiences through various organisations including CLT, CIOT, Mercia, MBL Seminars, SWAT UK, and the rural community direct.

Anna Coakes qualified as a solicitor in New South Wales in October 2003, joining a large regional firm advising on matrimonial and private client matters, including contentious trusts and estates. She moved to the UK in 2005, where she spent time working in the tax department of a large City firm, being admitted as a solicitor to the Law Society of England and Wales in 2006.

Anna moved to a West End firm in 2007 to advise on private client matters and she has continued to develop her private client practice since, focusing on the administration of complex estates and trusts for high net worth individuals, frequently involving complex multi-jurisdictional elements. Since January 2014, she has been an associate at Gordon Dadds LLP and continues to hold her practising certificate for New South Wales.

Anna has been a qualified Trusts and Estates Practitioner (TEP) since 2014, was shortlisted on the 2013 London Super Lawyers Rising Star list, and was recognised in Citywealth's Future Leaders List 2015. She regularly writes articles for various publications on private client matters and delivers presentations and seminars to trust professionals and family offices.

Penny Cogher, pensions partner at solicitors Irwin Mitchell, has nearly 25 years' experience in advising on the legal aspects of pensions. Her specialisms include advising on the complicated pension tax changes arising from the government's 2014, 2015, and 2016 pension changes. She advises both individuals and employers on the impact of these changes on high earners, and on how to reshape the high earner's remuneration package in a tax efficient way, including for example increasing the levels of life assurance and introducing excepted life assurance arrangements to top up the benefits payable on the death of key individuals.

Penny also advises on the successful resolution of pension disputes, many of which arise from partnerships or family arrangements going sour where the individuals have entered into small self-administered pension schemes (SSASs) or self-invested pension plans (SIPPs).

Pension sharing on divorce is another of Penny's areas of interest where the rules are currently changing to reflect the government's 2015 pension flexibilities. She understands the importance to both parties of achieving the right pension settlement. Additionally, Penny advises the trustees and employers of defined benefit and defined contribution schemes about all types of compliance.

Penny's services are provided at reasonable rates reflecting the fact that Irwin Mitchell is a truly national firm with many out of London offices.

Mark Davies is managing director and founder of Mark Davies & Associates, which he established in 2007 to focus on foreign domiciled persons who are resident in the UK. Mark trained with a Big 4 firm in Guernsey and has over 20 years of experience giving proactive tax advice with a personal touch.

Mark has regularly lectured on the subjects of residence and domicile. He is a co-author of chapters on tax planning for non-uk domiciled people and non-residents investing in the UK, which are published in *Tolley's Tax Planning*.

John Fitzgerald read Classics at the University of Oxford and obtained Masters degrees at Oxford and UCL in Classical

Archaeology and Forensic Archaeological Science respectively, before commencing his legal training at BPP University.

John joined Gordon Dadds LLP in September 2013 as a trainee solicitor and remained with the firm upon qualification in September 2015. He is a solicitor and member of the firm's Private Client and Dispute Resolution departments.

He advises on the drafting of wills for UK and non-UK based individuals, trust and estate administration, contentious probate and Inheritance Act claims, trust disputes, and claims involving breach of fiduciary duties. John is a student member of STEP and has written for various publications, including the *Solicitors Journal* and *The Times*.

Edward Hewitt has a traditional Chancery practice with a particular interest in private client work. He is regularly instructed in relation to challenges to the validity of wills, claims brought pursuant to the Inheritance (Provision for Family and Dependants) Act 1975, and all manner of trust disputes, both on and offshore, where he has appeared unled in the Grand Court of the Cayman Islands. He has experience in advising and acting in claims brought pursuant to the Variation of Trusts Act 1958, applications for directions as to the proper construction of wills and trust instruments, applications for the replacement of trustees and personal representatives, and disputes in the Court of Protection. He also undertakes a wide range of non-contentious drafting and advisory work in relation to wills, trusts, and estates and ancillary tax issues.

Outside the private client sphere, Edward's practice encompasses all areas of land law, insolvency law, and business disputes with a Chancery dimension. He is frequently instructed in relation to landlord and tenant disputes and proceedings involving the enforcement of mortgages and of all forms of property rights, particularly beneficial interests in land. In the insolvency context, Edward has experience advising and acting in all types of claims brought by liquidators and trustees in bankruptcy. Edward is a native Italian speaker and is often instructed in cases involving an Italian element.

Charlotte Kynaston is a barrister at Ten Old Square Chambers. She has a traditional Chancery practice with a focus on non-contentious private client work. She regularly advises on estate planning, capital taxation, and trust and estate administration. She is also experienced in drafting complex trust deeds.

Charlotte was recently seconded to the private client department of a major City firm, where she advised on the full spectrum of private client practice. She gained particular expertise in international private client taxation, trust administration, and probate matters.

Charlotte regularly writes articles and gives talks on issues relevant to her practice area. She assisted the editors of the most recent edition of *Williams on Wills*. Charlotte is a member of the Chancery Bar Association and a committee member of the Junior Chancery Bar Association. She is also an associate member of STEP, having gained a distinction in the STEP Advanced Certificate in UK Tax for International Clients.

Victoria Mahon de Palacios is a senior associate at Wedlake Bell LLP. Her practice includes all aspects of private client work. She has particular expertise in Court of Protection and vulnerable person's work to include advising on applications to the Court regarding deputyship appointments and widening of deputy's/attorney's powers to deal with an incapacitated person's assets, mental capacity issues, lasting/enduring powers of attorney, and protection of assets for vulnerable beneficiaries. Victoria's general practice also includes advising on methods of mitigating inheritance tax and capital gains tax through lifetime gifts, trusts, and tax-efficient wills, together with advising on the administering of estates and trusts. Victoria also advises on the establishment of new charitable structures, charity mergers, and variations to charitable trusts.

Victoria writes a quarterly column for *Solicitors Journal* on wealth management and is a contributing author to Lexis Nexis PSL's practice notes on lasting powers of attorney and issues relating to elderly clients. She has been named one of the country's 'Top 35 Under 35' private client advisers in *Private Client Practitioner* magazine for 2011, 2013, and 2014. Victoria is also a member of the Society of Trusts and Estates Practitioners (STEP) and the STEP Mental Capacity Special Interest Group.

Chris Moorcroft advises clients on international tax, succession planning, and trust matters. His clients include internationally mobile individuals with complex cross-border tax problems, frequently involving two or more high-tax jurisdictions. He advises on succession planning including the design of a wide range of sophisticated trust, foundation, and other estate planning structures, aimed to protect assets and facilitate the passing of wealth between generations. In addition, Chris also works with trust companies on the mitigation of fiduciary risk alongside other associated matters.

A significant element of his expertise involves advising UK and international high net worth individuals who are resident, investing, or spending time in UK on how to structure their assets. Chris also has experience in advising clients with US connections on estate planning matters. Chris was named on the *Private Client Practitioner* magazine's 'Top 35 Under 35' list for 2012 and 2013, which recognises the rising stars of the private client community.

Lisa Morgan is a partner with Hugh James. Lisa is the leading expert in NHS Continuing Healthcare and has been instrumental in developing a niche team of 90 lawyers specialising in the recovery of wrongly charged nursing care fees. The team has recovered in excess of £80 million on behalf of claimant families. Lisa won the prestigious and highly acclaimed Junior Lawyer of the Year at the Law Society's Excellence Awards in 2010.

The team at Hugh James acts for over 6,000 elderly clients

and families in England and Wales and their work has been highlighted in *Legal 500* which stated: 'Lisa Morgan's nursing care team is "second to none"', and 'Lisa Morgan was singled out for her "knowledge and tireless work" in nursing care'. Lisa is regularly turned to by the media as an expert the field and has undertaken numerous television and radio interviews for BBC News, BBC Breakfast, The One Show, ITV News, and BBC Radio.

Lisa lectures widely on the subject of continuing care to professionals and the voluntary sector and has also advised members of the Welsh Government on her experiences in challenging NHS decisions and the difficulties encountered by the elderly and their families in Wales in securing NHS funding. Since 2006, Lisa has also been the supervising solicitor for the award-winning Cardiff Law School's continuing healthcare pro bono scheme and a committee member for the South Wales' Solicitors for the Elderly Regional Group.

Ian Muirhead is a solicitor who began his professional career in the 1960s at City firm Norton Rose and subsequently went into industry as a legal adviser, personnel director, and company secretary. In the 1980s, he returned to private practice and became a partner in what is now TWM solicitors in Surrey, where he established an in-house financial services department. This led to interest in financial services on the part of other law firms and, in 1992, Ian set up SIFA (Solicitors Independent Financial Advice) to address this demand. SIFA now provides regulatory compliance, consultancy, and marketing services to firms of independent financial advisers and their solicitor connections. SIFA is recognised by the Law Society and the Financial Conduct Authority and its *Directory of Professional Financial Advisers* is endorsed by the Law Society. Ian is the author of the Law Society's handbook *Financial Services for Solicitors*, and of a range of client booklets and technical handbooks focusing on the connection between legal and financial services.

Sarah Sarwar is an associate in the Private Client Department at Druces. She has extensive experience in assisting individuals and families with their private client requirements.

Her work involves estate planning and succession issues, the creation of domestic and/or international trust and corporate structures, issues relating to residence and domicile, and philanthropy. This frequently involves complex tax advice with an international element and co-ordinating advice from advisors in different jurisdictions.

Her clients include multi-jurisdictional individuals, families, trustees, and beneficiaries, predominantly of high net worth and/or with business interests, residence and domicile considerations, or other complexities.

Sarah is a full member of the Society of Trust & Estate Practitioners (STEP), a worldwide recognised professional body admitting only the most experienced practitioners in the field of trusts and estates. She is also an elected committee member of the London Central Branch.

Sarah regularly gives seminars on private client law and practice and has contributed in many publications.

Martyn Wildney specialises in the field of private client tax and is a tax manager at Mark Davies & Associates. He enjoys helping individuals and their families to navigate the complexities of the UK tax system, with a particular focus on the needs of non-domiciled clients who are living in the UK or seeking to move to the UK.

He joined Mark Davies & Associates in May 2015 having experienced working in two Top 50 accountancy firms with a focus on international clients. Martyn graduated from Loughborough University with an Economics degree in 2007. He is a chartered tax adviser and a member of the Association of Taxation Technicians.

Chapter 1: Introduction – Major developments in private client practice

By Victoria Mahon de Palacios, senior associate at Wedlake Bell LLP

The private client landscape is ever changing. Since 2006 in particular, during and following which capital taxation has been subject to relentless change, the legal, tax, and wealth management issues for private client practitioners to tackle with and navigate their clients through continue to become increasingly complex. 2015 has certainly been no exception. Most notably, the Spring Budget in the lead-up to the general election and the all-Tory Summer Budget, following the Conservative election win, brought in a whole host of changes to the tax system, some anticipated while others were very much unexpected. A round-up of the most significant developments of 2015 in the private client arena are set out below, with more detail in the chapters that follow.

Inheritance tax developments

On the inheritance tax (IHT) front, three significant changes were introduced.

Residence nil rate band

Firstly, the introduction of the eagerly awaited residence nil rate band (RNRB) for the family home under the Finance (No. 2) Act 2015. With a view to easing the heavy burden of IHT on the family home on death due to increasing property values, the aim behind the RNRB is to allow the family home worth up to £1 million to pass on death free of IHT. The RNRB will be phased in for deaths from 6 April 2017, beginning at £100,000 and rising to £175,000 from 6 April 2020. It will be transferable between spouses/civil partners, bringing the total nil-rate band available to spouses/civil partners to £1 million between them from April 2020.

While an apparently simple concept, the detail in the new legislation shows otherwise. The family home must pass to 'direct descendants' (broadly, children or their spouses, civil partners, or widows/widowers), meaning childless couples cannot benefit, and will be tapered for those estates exceeding £2 million such that, from 2020/21, the allowance will be nil for estates worth in excess of £2.7 million (assuming the maximum transferable RNRB of £350,000 is available). In order not to dissuade individuals from downsizing, the government has also recently published provisions in the Finance Bill 2016 allowing those who downsize or cease to own a home from 8 July 2015 to still have use of that part of the nil rate band that they may have lost in doing so, provided that the smaller residence or assets of equivalent value are left to direct descendants.

An increase in the nil rate band is long overdue and so the RNRB is to be welcomed. However, the complexities in the new legislation, and the fact that it excludes certain estates from benefitting, leaves many questioning why the government did not simply increase the IHT nil rate band for the sake of simplicity and fairness.

Simplification of IHT charges on relevant property settlements

The goal of simplicity has been the focus of the government's second significant change in IHT – the long awaited proposed simplification of the complex IHT taxation of relevant property trusts (mooted by the government since 2012). However, the end result, in the form of the legislation introduced under the Finance (No.2) Act 2015, has instead added to the complexity. The most notable new provisions brought in are the 'same day addition' rules, which will largely put an end to the use of pilot trusts in tax planning for estates on death. Under these new rules, when calculating IHT charges on a trust (10 year anniversary charges and exit charges), additions made to other trusts on the same day as additions to the trust in question will be taken into account. This takes away the IHT benefit of pilot trusts set up on different days having their own nil rate bands for IHT relevant property purposes since, when assets are tipped into them on the same day (i.e. the date of death) from the deceased's estate, their values will effectively be aggregated for IHT purposes and will share a single nil-rate band. Pilot trusts referred to in wills prior to 10 December 2014 will be protected from these new rules if the testator dies before 6 April 2017. Pilot trusts created on different days that hold life insurance will not be affected if the policies have been correctly assigned to the trusts prior to the proceeds being paid out on death, as the lump sum pay-outs will not constitute additions.

Many practitioners breathed a heavy sigh of relief when the government announced their decision to scrap plans for the introduction of a single nil rate band to be shared between all trusts set up by one settlor as part of the proposed simplification. Also welcomed was the removal of the 'Frankland trap' which means that trustees of a relevant property trust can now make distributions out of the trust within three months of the testator's death without incurring an IHT exit charge, as the distributions will now be treated as if made by the testator for IHT purposes under section 144 of the Inheritance Tax Act 1984.

Disclosure of tax avoidance schemes

Meanwhile, private client practitioners will continue to be wary of the ever-widening net of the DOTAS (disclosure of tax avoidance schemes) regime so far as IHT is concerned. The third major move by the government in respect of IHT was the publication of very widely drawn draft regulations to bring more forms of IHT planning within the DOTAS regime. These were heavily criticised in the profession as potentially being able to catch any type of IHT planning, even the straightforward use of exemptions and reliefs. We hopefully await confirmation from HMRC that the draft regulations will be amended so as to be more tightly drawn.

Developments affecting non-doms and non-UK resident individuals

Taxation

2015 also proved to be an eventful year for non-UK domiciled and non-UK resident individuals who have been subject to extensive tax changes under the Finance Act 2015. Non-UK residents holding UK residential property have been the most affected in the light of the extension of capital gains tax (CGT) to disposals of such property as from 6 April 2015 (with the value of affected properties being rebased as at that date). Previously, non-UK residents were not liable to CGT on any of their UK gains. In a related step, the Finance Act 2015 also altered the principal private residence relief (PPR) rules in section 222 of the Taxation of Chargeable Gains Act 1992 to make it more difficult for non-UK residents to circumvent the new CGT charge by electing their UK property as their 'main residence' for PPR purposes. Under the new PPR rules, individuals must spend 90 days (which is generally assessed to be presence at the end of the day, i.e. midnight) during the tax year in the property in question or be tax resident in the country in which the property is located. The Annual Tax on Enveloped Dwellings (ATED) threshold was also lowered on the same date from £2 million to catch properties worth £1 million (to be lowered again on 6 April 2016 to £500,000), affecting many non-domiciled individuals with enveloped structures holding UK residential property, while the ATED annual chargeable amounts were increased at above inflation rates.

In addition to ATED increases, the Finance Act 2015 also increased the remittance basis charge (RBC) (the charge paid by non-UK domiciled, UK resident individuals to exclude their non-UK income and gains from UK taxation) so that, as from 6 April 2015, this is now £60,000 for individuals who have been UK resident in 12 or more of the 14 tax years before the year of claim and £90,000 for those who have been UK resident in 17 or more of the 20 tax years before the year of claim.

Domicile

Hot on the heels of the aforementioned changes, the government then announced a radical overhaul of the core principles of the taxation of non-domiciled individuals in its Summer Budget. Three principal changes have been proposed which have since been undergoing or awaiting consultation.

Firstly, the abolition of permanent non-domiciled status for tax purposes. Instead, the government's consultation paper (published on 30 September 2015) proposed that non-domiciled individuals will be treated as deemed UK domiciled for tax purposes once they have resided in the UK for 15 out of the previous 20 years. Briefly, this will mean that long-term non-UK domiciled individuals will no longer be able to opt to be taxed on the remittance basis in respect of their offshore income and gains and their worldwide assets will be subject to IHT. It is proposed that time spent by a child in the UK will count as part of their 15 year clock – an element of the proposals that has been subject to criticism within the profession.

Secondly, individuals born in the UK with a UK domicile of origin who later acquire a non-UK domicile of choice, having moved abroad, will immediately be deemed to be domiciled in the UK upon their return to the UK and re-acquiring UK residency. Interestingly, the proposal is not intended to affect individuals born overseas with a UK domicile of origin.

Thirdly, the Summer Budget also announced the final blow to offshore structures holding UK residential property, already heavily beaten of late, in that they are to come within the UK IHT net from which they are currently sheltered. We currently await a consultation on this third aspect of the reforms.

It is intended that the legislation will be finalised in 2016 with the new rules to come into force from 6 April 2017. Given the intricate complexities in drafting legislation to introduce such radical changes, and the need to address complex existing anti-avoidance provisions (not least the effect of the 15/20 rule on the taxation of remittance basis users and recipients of distributions from offshore trusts), many responses to the consultation have requested that the government delay the introduction of the new rules by another year to give itself more time to carefully consider such issues. This would also allow non-UK domiciled individuals time to re-structure their affairs in time for the proposed changes. We wait to hear the government's response to the first consultation, which is expected in early 2016.

Closure of Liechtenstein Disclosure Facility

Also on the offshore front, we saw the early closure of the over six-year-long Liechtenstein Disclosure Facility (LDF) at the end of 2015 (instead of the proposed April 2016 closure). This had been the most prominent disclosure facility in the last few years, enabling persons with unreported liabilities relating to assets held overseas to settle them with HMRC on favourable terms. Although the LDF has (as from 1 January 2016) closed, it is being replaced with a new disclosure facility for a limited time only (running between 2016 and 2017), which imposes higher penalties than the LDF and offers no immunity from prosecution in respect of previously unpaid taxes that the LDF offered. This is intended to be the final disclosure opportunity for anyone with undeclared offshore income and gains to come forward before the government becomes increasingly aggressive towards tax evaders when it starts to receive information under the Common Reporting Standard (CRS) which affects accounts with UK financial institutions in existence at 31 December 2015 and new accounts opened from 1 January 2016, albeit the first reporting to HMRC is not due until 31 May 2017.

Common reporting standard

No sooner had tax authorities and financial institutions got to grips with the complex technicalities of the Foreign Account Tax Compliance Act (FATCA), introduced by the US to encourage better tax compliance, they are now having to digest the requirements of further increased reporting obligations under the far more wide reaching common reporting standard

(CRS). The CRS, which has secured widespread global participation, marks a significant step towards ensuring global tax compliance. Under it, the participating countries, including the UK, will receive much more information about their taxpayer's overseas assets and income through obtaining information from their financial institutions and exchanging them with other nations, building upon the framework of information sharing brought about by FATCA and the European Union Savings Directive. The CRS will be one of the major new regimes that financial institutions, their customers and/or beneficiaries, and those in the private client industry that advise them, will need to get to grips with during the course of 2016.

Trust developments

Trust register: Fourth European AML Directive

The move towards greater cross-border information sharing is also extending to trusts. The government published a 'plan' in Autumn 2015 showing how the UK will implement the G20 principles on beneficial ownership transparency. The proposals are timetabled to be included in the UK's anti-money laundering regulations in 2017 that will implement the Fourth Money Laundering EU Directive. In line with the Directive, the government will be requiring trustees to hold information about the settlor, trustees, and beneficaries of express trusts and will be establishing a central register to hold beneficial ownership information of trusts that generate tax consequences in the UK; such information can then be accessed by relevant domestic authorities.

It has not yet been clarified what is meant by 'tax consequences', albeit it is likely that any UK tax consequence made by a trust will be included. It is envisaged that offshore trusts with UK tax-paying beneficiaries will be caught. The original intention for a trust register to be made public has thankfully been removed under the Directive due to concerns rasied in the UK private client profession over potential risks posed to vulnerable beneficiaries. We are yet to see whether the register will be linked to other EU member state's trust registers and accessed via a centrally held EU register by relevant foreign authorities.

Estate developments

EU Succession Regulation

Significant recent developments in the cross border arena are not only confined to tax and trust issues; Europe witnessed a revolution in EU succession law with the introduction of the EU Succession Regulation, colloquially known as Brussels IV, on 17 August 2015. This brings in new rules to determine which country's laws govern the succession to an individual's estate on death. Under Brussels IV, any assets located in an EU member state (excluding the UK, Ireland, and Denmark who have not signed up to the Regulation), will now devolve on death under the succession laws of the country where the deceased was habitually resident unless the deceased had made an election in their will for the law of the country of which they were a national to apply. This has a significant impact on UK nationals who have assets in the EU or are resident in an EU member state by offering them the freedom to control how their estate devolves and potentially avoid forced heirship laws of foreign countries.

Although Brussels IV is intended to simplify cross-border succession, it did not come without its uncertainties for the UK private client profession. A question mark remains over whether the UK is a 'third' or 'member' state under the Regulation. This is important in determining whether the notoriously complex concept of 'renvoi' (in short, the process by which a court adopts the rules of a foreign jurisdiction with respect to any conflict of laws that arises) applies when the governing law is that of habitual residence. Practitioners have also been questioning whether a non-UK domiciled UK citizen making an election for UK law to apply to their estate will cause the Inheritance (Provision for Family and Dependants) Act 1975 to be applicable to their estate. There is also concern over whether elections will be recognised by local notaries if it means forced heirship will be avoided. Time will tell if these uncertainties will be ironed out during the course of the current year or those following.

Inheritance (Provision for Family and Dependants) Act 1975 ('the 1975 Act')

Turning closer to home, one of the most significant and widely reported cases of 2015 was that of *Ilott v Milson* [2015] EWCA Civ 797 described by the press as opening the floodgates to more claims being brought against estates under the 1975 Act for financial provision by dissatisfied relatives and undermining the principle of testamentary freedom. In this case, the deceased's only daughter successfully challenged her late mother's will which left her estate to charity so that she was awarded a one-third share in the estate. Successful claims by able bodied adults who can earn their own living, such as the daughter in the *Ilott* case, have previously been limited.

While this case does show that able-bodied adults can bring successful claims against estates for financial provision, each case will depend on its individual facts. In the *Ilott* case, the fact that the deceased had little connection to the charities she named in her will and apparently no good reason to exclude her daughter from benefit, tied in with the fact that her daughter would face poverty without financial provision, while the animal charities named in the will had no such human need, were significant in the court reaching its decision. While the case should not open the floodgates as such, it is likely to encourage individuals who may be on the breadline to consider making claims for financial provision against a deceased relative's estate and should encourage testators to think more carefully about their reasons for excluding family members from benefit.

Developments affecting the elderly/ those lacking capacity

A welcome improvement in the process of appointing someone to manage an individual's financial affairs and make decisions regarding their health and welfare in the event that they may lack capacity to do so themselves in the future, came about by the Office of the Public Guardian's introduction of new lasting power of attorney (LPA) forms on 1 July 2015. The shorter, more user-friendly forms that do away with some of the previous formalities for making an LPA have significantly simplified the LPA making process, benefitting clients and advisers alike.

On the care front, the Care Act 2014 partially came into force on 1 April 2015, heralding the most important change to adult social care since the National Assistance Act 1948. Part 1 of the Act, which is now in force, sets out the provisions relevant to those advising individuals on planning for and funding long-term care.

The most notable feature of the Act for many is the introduction of a single legal framework for charging for care. As part of this, a cap of £72,000 on the amount that an individual must pay towards their care costs was to be brought in under the second phase of provisions under the Act in April 2016. This has since been postponed until April 2020 due to concerns over how the cap will be funded. The introduction of an increase in capital limits below which an individual will not have to fund care costs has also been delayed until 2020.

Commentators have widely questioned the benefit of the proposed cap due to the fact that it is likely to never be reached in the light of there being restrictions over what care costs count towards the cap and the relatively short life expectancy of care home residents. In any event, there are rising concerns that the proposed care cap will not be introduced even by 2020, or indeed at all, as it is not clear how the government will fund it. We will watch this space.

Chapter 2: **Giving with one hand and taking away with the other – Recent developments in inheritance tax legislation**

By Charlotte Kynaston, barrister at Ten Old Square

Recent research into public opinion on taxation concluded that inheritance tax remains almost universally unpopular, even among those whose estates are unlikely to ever be subject to the tax.[1] Participants in the research felt that the inheritance tax burden fell unfairly on people with modest incomes who had worked hard to pass money on to their children, while those wealthy enough could 'get around' inheritance tax with clever planning.

While the rate of inheritance tax and the level of the nil-rate band have remained unchanged for many years,[2] the government this year announced more minor changes to the inheritance tax legislation to address these perceived problems with the system. The apparent intention is to reduce the inheritance tax burden on parents with modest estates while removing planning opportunities to avoid inheritance tax.

This analysis will consider the 'winners' and 'losers' of these changes, and how practitioners will need to advise their clients in light of them.

Winners?

(i) Generous parents: Residence nil-rate band

The biggest 'winners' of the last Finance Act are those who will benefit from the residence nil-rate band (RNRB), to take effect from 6 April 2017.[3] Many clients will have seen newspaper headlines proclaiming that the RNRB means married couples will now be able to pass on £1 million tax free.[4] The headlines are not wholly inaccurate. When it first applies in 2017, the

RNRB will be worth a maximum of £100,000 per person, increasing up to £175,000 in April 2020. As the RNRB is transferable between spouses, that could give a married couple a RNRB of £350,000 in addition to their £650,000 nil-rate band.

The full story, however, is rather more complex and restricted. Practitioners are likely to have to explain to many disappointed clients that they will not benefit from the RNRB.

Who will benefit from the RNRB?

(a) Estates below £2 million: The most significant restriction in the legislation is that the full RNRB will only be available to estates worth £2 million or less. The RNRB tapers by £1 for every £2 the estate is worth above that limit, so that in 2017 an estate worth £2.2 million will have no RNRB at all.

For some married couples with joint marital assets worth more than £2 million, the estate of the first spouse to die will nonetheless be under £2 million. While there is no way to make use of both RNRBs, it may be possible to make use at least of the first spouse's RNRB on their death, and to reduce the overall inheritance tax on the marital assets. However, practitioners will need to be sensitive about this type of planning, as it will usually require some of the marital home to be passed on to children, whether outright or in trust. In many cases, practical considerations will outweigh the relatively small inheritance tax saving possible.

(b) Home owners (or former home owners): The next restriction in the legislation is that the estate must contain a 'qualifying residential interest' (QRI). The amount of the RNRB is restricted to the value of the QRI.

A QRI is an interest in a dwelling-house which the deceased has resided in. There is no requirement that the deceased still resides in the property, so the definition would include (for example) a home abroad in which the deceased used to live. If an estate contains more than one

QRI, the personal representatives can choose which QRI the RNRB attaches to.

Initially, there was concern that the RNRB would discourage people from downsizing or selling their homes to pay care home fees. If they downsized, the QRI in their estate would be much smaller and if they sold their home they would have no QRI at all. The Draft Finance Bill 2016 contains provisions to address this concern, which are intended to come into effect in April 2017, at the same time as the RNRB.[5] The draft legislation allows estates with 'former qualifying residential interests' to benefit from the RNRB.

The provisions will not solve the problem completely. The inevitable downside is that the value of the home will be 'locked in' at the date of the sale, regardless of the increase in property prices to the date of death. Further, the provisions will not apply to any home sold before 8 July 2015, so some people who have already downsized will miss out on the RNRB.

(c) Parents: The final significant restriction is that the QRI (or at least some of it) must be inherited by a lineal descendant or the spouse of a lineal descendant. While this sounds simple, it becomes more complicated if there are any trusts involved.

If the deceased owns the QRI absolutely, they can either leave it to their lineal descendant absolutely, or grant the lineal descendant a qualifying interest in possession for inheritance tax purposes (which, in practice, will usually be an immediate post death interest in possession). However, if the deceased only has a qualifying interest in possession in the QRI, it appears likely from the draft legislation that it must pass to the lineal descendant absolutely if the estate is to benefit from the RNRB.

Difficulties with the legislation

The above analysis will give a sense of the difficulties of the legislation. What could have been simple has become excessively complex because of the insistence that the RNRB is restricted to a narrow class of estates.

While it is easy to understand why the government wishes high value estates to be excluded from the RNRB, the reasoning behind the other restrictions is less clear. People who have rented property throughout their lives, or who are childless, could fairly ask why they are being prevented from benefiting from the RNRB.

There have been calls for the RNRB as currently enacted to be replaced by a simple additional nil-rate band of £100,000 which tapers where the estate is worth more than £2 million. So far, these suggestions have fallen on deaf ears. Practitioners will need to be ready to guide their clients through the labyrinth of the legislation.

(ii) All estates: Deeds of variation

Those using deeds of variation were nearly early 'losers' in the drive to reduce inheritance tax avoidance, after George Osborne announced a consultation into their use for tax purposes in March. Since 1972, deeds of variation have been used to alter the distribution of an estate for inheritance tax (or estate tax, as it then was) purposes.[6] Given this long history, it was hoped by many practitioners that George Osborne's announcement was simply an easy jibe at Ed Miliband, who (it was reported) benefited from a deed of variation altering the distribution of his father's estate.

The responses to the consultation were emphatic in their support for deeds of variation. Out of 214 respondents, only two argued that the use of deeds of variation for tax purposes should be restricted. Many respondents emphasised that deeds of variation only allowed beneficiaries to do what the deceased themselves could have done, had they been properly advised before their death. Restricting the use of deeds of variation would penalise those who could not afford to seek extensive tax planning advice, or who had not had a chance to update their will following changes to family circumstances.[7]

The government accepted the overwhelming feeling of the respondents and confirmed that, at present, it is not planning any restrictions on deeds of variation. This must be good news for all estates.

Losers?

(i) Settlors of pilot trusts

Perhaps unsurprisingly, the main 'losers' of the last Finance Act were those intending to use pilot trusts to reduce inheritance tax on their trusts after death. Previously, it was possible for a testator to set up lifetime trusts with nominal capital, and to leave funds to each trust in their will. A lacuna in the legislation meant that the additions to the other trusts would not be taken into account when calculating anniversary and exit inheritance tax charges for each trust.

The government initially proposed a complete change to the system of trust taxation.[8] Every settlor would have (in addition to their nil-rate band) a settlement nil-rate band to be split between all their trusts, whether settled during their lifetime or in their will. The settlor (or their personal representatives) could choose to split the settlement nil-rate band between the trusts in whatever proportion they chose. As well as closing the pilot trust loophole, this would also have prevented the practice of individuals settling property up to the value of the nil-rate band into trust every seven years.

In the end, the government decided to tweak the existing system of relevant property trust taxation rather than overhaul it. The new legislation is targeted at the specific issue of pilot trusts.[9] It requires trustees calculating anniversary and exit charges to take into account the value of other settlements into which property was added on the same day.

The legislation applies not only to all trusts created on or after 10 December 2014, but also to all trusts with property added after that date (unless the property was added on the settlor's death before 6 April 2016, as a result of provisions in their will dating from before 10 December 2014). Clients relying on pilot trusts will need to be advised that this planning will no longer work, so that they can reconsider their estate planning options.

(ii) Non-domiciliaries: Deemed domicile rules

The principal 'losers' of the draft Finance Bill 2016 look set to be non-domiciliaries, more of whom will be required to pay UK inheritance tax on their worldwide assets. The general rule is that if an individual is domiciled in any part of the UK, UK inheritance tax is due on their worldwide assets (subject to double tax treaties and unilateral relief). If they are not domiciled in the UK, inheritance tax is only due on their UK assets. However, there is a class of people who are deemed to be domiciled in the UK, regardless of their domicile status under the general law.

The Draft Finance Bill 2016 introduces two changes to the class of people who are deemed to be domiciled in the UK for inheritance tax purposes.[10]

15/20 year rule

The first change is a relatively minor tweak to the current deemed domicile rules. A UK resident will now become deemed domiciled for inheritance tax purposes after being resident in the UK for 15 of the past 20 tax years, rather than 17 of the past 20 tax years as previously. This change will bring the deemed domicile provisions for inheritance tax in line with the newly announced deemed domicile provisions for income tax and capital gains tax.

As well as making UK residents deemed domiciled more quickly, the 15/20 year rule will also mean they remain deemed domiciled until they have been non-UK resident for a full five tax years.

The reduction in the time it takes to become deemed domiciled could come as an unwelcome surprise to those already resident in the UK, as there are no grandfathering provisions in the legislation. However, the legislation is still in draft form and will not come into effect until 6 April 2017. Practitioners still have time to advise their non-domiciled clients on how best to arrange their affairs, including transferring assets to an excluded property trust if appropriate.

The 'formerly domiciled resident' rule

The second proposed change creates a whole new class of deemed domiciliaries – the 'formerly domiciled resident'. This new category appears to have been proposed largely as a response to the public outcry over the tax affairs of Stuart Gulliver, the chief executive of HSBC. It emerged that Mr Gulliver was claiming a domicile of choice in Hong Kong while living in the UK, despite having been born and raised in the UK.

A formerly domiciled resident is not any resident formerly domiciled in the UK under the general law, but only a person born in the UK with a UK domicile of origin. Given that a person's domicile of origin is based on their father's domicile at the time of their birth (or their mother's if their parents are unmarried), there may be some clients who will have to consider carefully their parents' domicile at the time of their birth, to see if they come within this definition.

Formerly domiciled residents will be deemed domiciled in the UK provided they are UK resident and have been resident for just one out of the past two tax years. Practitioners will need to consider whether any of their clients fall within the definition of a formerly domiciled resident, as this proposed change will have a significant impact on them.

It is doubtful how many clients this will affect in practice, however. HMRC usually take a fairly aggressive stance towards questionable claims that an individual is non-domiciled. It is unlikely that many UK residents who were born in the UK with a UK domicile of origin have successfully claimed non-domiciled status.

(iii) Trustees of excluded property trusts

The other potential 'losers' of the new formerly domiciled resident rule are the trustees of excluded property trusts with formerly domiciled residents as settlors. At present, excluded property trusts set up by non-domiciled individuals remain outside of the UK inheritance tax net even if the settlor subsequently becomes UK domiciled or deemed domiciled.

Under the proposed changes, a trust settled by a formerly domiciled resident while they were non-domiciled will cease to be an excluded property trust when they become deemed domiciled. When the settlor leaves the UK and ceases to be deemed domiciled, the trust will revert to being an excluded property trust.

This means that the trust may become subject to a 10-yearly inheritance tax charge while the settlor is deemed domiciled in the UK. This could cause difficulties for the trustees. They may not know that the settlor has become deemed domiciled, and that the trust is liable to pay the 10-year charge. Even if they do, the trustees may not have kept sufficient records to enable them to calculate the charge.

If the proposed legislation does become law as currently envisaged, trustees will have to keep a close eye on any settlors who were born in the UK with a UK domicile of origin. They may need to keep detailed records from the settlement of the trust, in case the trust does become subject to the relevant property regime at a later date.

(iv) Offshore companies which own UK residential property

At the same time as announcing the changes to the deemed domicile rules, the government also announced an intention to ensure that all UK residential property is subject to inheritance tax, even property held through an offshore company.[11] The government has not yet produced any draft legislation, and there is a chance it will not do so. However, the proposed change would be in keeping with the hostile approach to enveloped residential dwellings shown in the last few years by the introduction of ATED, ATED CGT, and the higher rate of SDLT.

When combined with those other taxes, the loss of inheritance tax benefits might be the final nail in the coffin in the use of offshore companies to hold UK residential properties. While privacy and asset protection will still be important concerns, many clients will be better advised to own residential property personally.

Conclusions

The recent changes to inheritance tax legislation have been driven by sensible motivations, and have removed some temptations towards aggressive planning. If the government's intention was to shift more of the inheritance tax burden onto the wealthiest, they have probably achieved it.

However, the continual amendments to the inheritance tax legislation are only serving to further complicate an already complicated system. Most individuals have little hope of navigating their way through the legislation. There is a risk that the real winners of all the recent changes will be the practitioners advising on inheritance tax, and the real losers those who cannot afford that advice.

References

1. Srblin, D., 'The Tax Detox: Winning public consent for radical tax reform', Fabian Society, December 2015; available at: www.fabians.org.uk/wp-content/uploads/2015/12/The-Tax-Detox.pdf
2. The inheritance tax rate has been 40 per cent since its inception in 1988, and the nil-rate band has been set at £325,000 since 6 April 2009.
3. Introduced in Finance (No. 2) Act 2015, section 9.
4. For example, the *Independent* had 'Inheritance tax threshold "raised" above £1m for couples by new Family Homes Allowance'; see: www.independent.co.uk/news/business/news/budget-2015-live-emergency-uk-inheritance-tax-threshold-raised-above-1m-for-couples-by-new-family-10370076.html.
5. Draft Finance Bill 2016, section 44.
6. Inheritance Tax Act 1984, section 142.
7. HMRC, 'Review of Deeds of Variation for Tax Purposes – Call for Evidence' (summary of responses), December 2015; available at: www.gov.uk/government/uploads/system/uploads/attachment_data/file/483388/Review_of_Deeds_of_Variation_for_Tax_Purposes_-_summary_of_responses__M7046_.pdf.
8. HMRC, 'Inheritance tax: A fairer way of calculating trust charges' (consultation document), 6 June–29 August 2014; available at:

www.gov.uk/government/uploads/system/uploads/attachment_data/file/317871/140605_Final.pdf.

9. Finance (No. 2) Act 2015, section11 and schedule 1.
10. Draft Finance Bill 2016, section 43.
11. HMRC, 'Summer Budget 2015', available at: www.gov.uk/government/publications/summer-budget-2015/summer-budget-2015.

Chapter 3:
Non-Doms – The end of the permanent non-dom and other changes

By Chris Moorcroft, senior associate at Harbottle & Lewis LLP

The UK tax regime for wealthy non-domiciled individuals, particularly those who are or become resident in the UK, is currently extremely uncertain. The rules are subject to frequent change, creating a problem for individuals who have based themselves in Britain at least in part because of its relative stability.

'Non-dom' status has become heavily politicised. In a country grappling with a vast national deficit and a public perception of increasing inequality, fuelled in part by ever increasing house prices, a small block of wealthy foreign individuals make an easy target both for finger pointing and revenue raising. Only the fear of a mass exodus of wealthy foreigners, taking their tax receipts and business with them, prevents the changes from being even more drastic.

It is therefore becoming increasingly difficult to advise individuals on their tax status with the constantly changing nature of the law concerning the treatment of non-doms. Some of the most significant changes made over the past year are summarised in this article.

Changes to the remittance basis

The Summer Budget 2015 saw the government announce a major overhaul of the remittance basis of taxation. The basic proposal is that the ability to claim the remittance basis will now be restricted for the following individuals from April 2017.

Firstly, there is a change to the old domicile rule for a person who was born in the UK with a domicile in one of the countries forming the UK and who then acquired a domicile somewhere else after having left the UK. Should that person later return to the UK, it is proposed that a new deeming rule will effectively re-instate their original domicile in the UK for tax purposes on their return.

The second is a deemed domicile provision for all UK tax purposes. Where an individual has been resident in the UK for 15 years as of 6 April 2017, the person will be deemed to be UK domiciled for all UK tax purposes starting at that fifteenth year. This new rule effectively overrides the current 17-out-of-20 years deeming rules for inheritance tax (IHT) purposes. Individuals that fall into either of the above two categories will not be able to claim the remittance basis of taxation after April 2017, which means that their worldwide income and gains will become subject to UK income and capital gains tax (CGT), regardless of whether or not it is brought to the UK. The deemed domicile rules for IHT purposes will also be aligned with the new rules.

As would be expected, those who have held non-dom status for a number of years have already begun to consider the implications for their tax affairs in response to these changes. Many long-term non-doms will presumably now consider the option to become non-resident before 6 April 2017, or at the very least to become non-resident prior to triggering a deemed domicile status in the UK.

The details published by HMRC do, however, leave it possible for individuals in the second category to plan their affairs using trusts before they reach 15 years of residence (or before April 2017, whichever is later). Such a move is a big boost to the offshore trusts industry. It appears that those who set up an offshore trust before they become deemed domiciled will not be taxed on trust income and gains that are retained in the trust and such trusts will have the same IHT treatment as at present. There will however be UK tax charges where distributions are made from such trusts, either to the settlor themselves or their spouse or children.

Our view is that the design of these changes has been shrewd. For those considering moving to the UK, it will be unlikely that the changes will deter them, as 15 years of the remittance basis remains generous. Likewise, those whose residence is approaching 15 years will generally have established significant ties to the UK, so relatively few may choose to leave, especially given the opportunity for them to use effective offshore trust planning before this time.

IHT residential property changes

Another very significant change announced in the Summer Budget 2015 is targeted directly at UK residential property ownership. Put simply, under the proposal, offshore companies and certain other vehicles holding UK residential property will now be transparent for IHT purposes. This is regardless of the value of the property, whether it is occupied by the beneficial owner or commercially rented out, and regardless of whether or not the annual tax on enveloped dwellings (ATED) is already paid in respect of the property.

For individuals owning such companies in their own name, the proposed changes will now simply bring the value of the property within the scope of UK IHT. The death of the owner of the shares in the company will therefore become an event which is potentially chargeable to IHT, albeit that the document issued by the government indicates that normal reliefs and exemptions will apply. Therefore any transfer of the company shares to the spouse of the individuals should normally be relievable by virtue of the spouse exemption and IHT-free, and debt which is secured against the property by the company should in some cases be deductible against the value of the property (although we will need to see the design of the legislation to understand exactly how this will work).

The second major impact will be for trusts which own the shares of non-UK companies which own UK residential property. In this scenario, the effect of making the companies transparent for IHT purposes will be to bring the property within the rules that currently apply to direct trust ownership of UK property by offshore trustees. This will have the following consequences:

- Trusts will be subject to IHT charges on their 10 year anniversaries, based on the value of the underlying UK property;
- Distributions of UK property from the trust may become subject to exit charges; and
- The gift with reservation of benefit rules will be in point, such that if the settlor, their spouse, or any minor children of the settlor are beneficiaries of the trust (which will be the case in the majority of cases), those trusts will be subject to IHT on the death of the settlor as though the settlor owned the property in their personal name.

These changes are significant for many. Coming so soon after ATED, it is likely that clients will again have to carefully consider their options and re-visit the reasoning for setting up the structure in the first place. Some will want to unwind structures, but they may find that the costs of unwinding are very significant indeed.

This is an absolutely critical point. Some clients chose not to 'de-envelop' at the time ATED was introduced because the tax costs of doing so were too great. The costs were generally of two types: SDLT on the value of debt which could not be refinanced; or CGT charges (usually under the section 87 matching rules), which would be triggered by virtue of the restructuring. Those potential costs are unlikely to have disappeared since the introduction of ATED and will now frequently be joined by a third, 'ATED-related CGT' – which formed part of the ATED suite of taxes introduced in 2013 – and a fourth, 'non-residents CGT', introduced in 2015.

Importantly, the technical briefing note hints at the possibility of some sort of moratorium on tax costs of unwinding the structure, although no detail is given. This needs to be monitored. It is an issue of fundamental importance because the government needs to provide an escape route for clients who could otherwise be locked into structures which they cannot afford. However, even where the structure can be unwound tax efficiently, there are still significant costs of tax advice, property lawyers, and other professional costs (such as those of the trustee, liquidator etc.) which must be factored in.

In discussing all of the many tax complexities that surround this area, the non-tax reasons for such structures can easily be forgotten. However, in very many cases structures will have been established for non-tax reasons and it is critical that these considerations (such as succession planning and confidentiality) are included and put at the forefront of any decisions which are taken.

Collateral

Following last summer's abrupt change in HMRC policy on resident non-domiciled individuals that take loans using unremitted foreign income or gains as collateral, in a further development on 15 October 2015, HMRC announced a partial backtrack. Loans taken out by remittance basis users before 4 August 2014 will now continue to benefit from the previous concessionary treatment.

By way of reminder, it was previously possible for a resident non-domiciled individual (RND) to obtain a loan from a bank, secured on their non-UK income/gains. There was disagreement among the profession as to whether or not such a loan might itself cause a taxable remittance, but HMRC's approach had always been very clear: provided that the loan was serviced (in respect of interest and the like) out of clean capital sources, there was no taxable remittance. As a consequence, large numbers of RNDs relied on HMRC's position and entered into such loan arrangements with banks to fund their UK spending.

On 4 August 2014, however, HMRC changed its mind; in the opinion of HMRC, using non-UK income/gains as security does now trigger a taxable remittance. In addition, RNDs were given until April 2016 to either repay the loans or offer alternative security and, to make matters worse, RNDs were told also to provide details of all such existing loans to HMRC.

The development on 15 October 2015 represented a partial backtrack. HMRC will not now require loans taken out prior to the 4 August announcement to be refinanced and will not treat the collateral as being remitted, although going forward this strategy will remain ineffective for new loans.

This policy review follows heavy criticism from representative bodies that re-structuring such arrangements and replacing them with non-foreign income and gains collateral would have been costly, difficult, and unfair due to the retrospective nature of the change.

Additional SDLT

As announced in the Autumn Statement 2015, higher rates of SDLT will be charged on purchases of additional residential properties (above £40,000), such as buy-to-let properties and second homes, from 1 April 2016.

The higher rates will be 3 per cent above the current SDLT rates; however, the increased rates will not apply to purchases of caravans, mobile homes, or houseboats, or to corporates or funds making significant investments in residential property given the role of this investment in supporting the government's housing agenda. The government is consulting on the policy detail in early 2016, including on whether an exemption for corporates and funds owning more than 15 residential properties is appropriate.

Importantly, this change will also affect overseas buyers looking to purchase additional property in the UK. Where an individual owns a property overseas and wishes to buy a property which will not be their main residence, that UK property will also be subject to the 3 per cent increase.

This change will have a further significant impact on the UK residential property market, particularly in London, and particularly of the most expensive properties. Coming on the back of ATED, non-residents CGT, and the impending change in IHT treatment discussed above, many wealthy foreigners will be put off buying London properties. Such an impact may well be intended.

Conclusions

The tax world has changed enormously over the last few years, and in political terms, few people represent such an as easy a target as non-doms. For that reason, and in light of the many changes that have happened in this area, all non-doms (but particularly those with more complicated affairs) should consider 'health-checking' their tax planning. Everyone needs to assess whether they need to arrange their affairs to reflect the new UK tax environment and consequent level of tax exposure and risk. The boundaries have shifted enormously; tax planning once considered benign may no longer be viewed as such by HMRC. It is far better to be ahead of the curve than trailing behind it.

Chapter 4:
Clean capital

By Martyn Wildney, tax manager, and Mark Davies, managing director, at Mark Davies & Associates

One of the defining features of the UK's tax regime for UK resident foreign domiciliaries (or 'non-doms') is the ability to access the remittance basis of taxation.

Unlike ordinary UK domiciled residents, who are taxable on their worldwide income and gains on an arising basis, UK resident non-doms can elect to be taxed on the remittance basis instead. In some cases it also applies automatically. Where the remittance basis applies for a particular tax year, an individual remains taxable on any UK source income or gains that arise, but their foreign income and gains are only taxable if, and to the extent that, they are 'remitted' to the UK (i.e. used in, or brought to, or enjoyed in the UK).

Therefore, on general principles, the remittance basis becomes more attractive where taxable remittances can be minimised. The most obvious way of avoiding a taxable remittance is to simply avoid remitting money to the UK. However, this is seldom realistic, and the next best solution is often to ensure that any money that is brought to the UK is not subject to tax. Funds of this kind held overseas by a UK resident non-dom, representing neither foreign income nor gains, are commonly referred to as 'clean capital'.

In essence, the object of managing clean capital is to maximise the benefits of the remittance basis, and thus it is a central component of UK tax planning for non-doms. The legislation governing remittances and remittances from mixed funds (see below) is complex. While there are various tax planning considerations for non-doms, this chapter is wholly concerned with the planning methods and considerations relevant to ensuring that a non-UK domiciled individual is able to bring money to the UK in a tax efficient way.

Definition of clean capital

It is important to understand exactly what is meant by clean capital from a tax perspective. This is not a concept defined anywhere in statute and it has a very limited meaning.

Clean capital can arise from:

1. Inheritance;
2. Gifts; and
3. Foreign income and gains arising before an individual becomes UK tax resident.

However, there are important caveats to be aware of in respect of each of these sources of clean capital.

Inheritance

It is sometimes, but not always, the case that an inheritance represents clean capital in the hands of the recipient. Where an inheritance has been received by a non-dom and the intention is to remit those funds to the UK, further questions should be asked to determine whether or not this will in fact give rise to a UK tax liability.

Assuming there is income within the estate, the first consideration should be the residence of the estate, since this will determine the source of the estate income. If the estate is considered to be a UK estate then UK inheritance tax may be due, but no further income tax or capital gains tax will be due on the capital received by the legatee and it is a case of quantifying any income arising during the course of the administration of the estate which might be taxable.

If the individual is the beneficiary of a foreign estate, then it is necessary to confirm their entitlement. Where a legacy is received, this will be mostly of a capital nature, subject to any income element paid by the executors. However, where the individual has a residuary interest in the estate, income arising during the administration period may, depending on the circumstances, attach to distributions they receive.

Gifts

In relation to cash gifts from individuals, it should be borne in mind that while the subsequent remittance of these monies will not create a UK tax liability for the donee, it could potentially create a UK tax liability for the donor if the donee was a 'relevant person' in relation to them (section 809M, ITA 2007). Relevant persons include an individual's spouse, minor children, and minor grandchildren. More remote relatives are not caught, nor are adult children/grandchildren.

However, the anti-avoidance provisions conditions C and D (section 809L, ITA 2007) should also be considered. Sometimes referred to as the 'gift recipient' rules, these provisions are designed to ensure that a taxable remittance arises where the taxpayer 'enjoys' property in the UK which belongs to another person (who is not the taxpayer or a relevant person) and the enjoyed property represents, or was derived from, foreign income or gains originally gifted from the taxpayer to the owner.

This would, for example, prevent a father from making a gift of cash representing his foreign income and gains to his adult son offshore, and then subsequently enjoying the cash (or other property derived from it) in the UK without creating a taxable remittance.

Notably, if the taxpayer and/or relevant persons are virtually excluded from enjoying the property or full consideration is given for that enjoyment then it is disregarded. However, 'enjoyment' is not defined anywhere in the legislation and so it is difficult to know precisely where the boundaries lie in the eyes of HM Revenue & Customs (HMRC). It is prudent to ensure that no benefit whatsoever is derived by the taxpayer or other relevant persons if it is thought that the gift recipient rules could apply.

Pre-arrival foreign income and gains

It is a key feature of the remittance basis that foreign income and gains arising before an individual becomes UK resident are not taxable in the UK if subsequently remitted to the UK. Notably, pre-arrival income and gains do not need to be remitted to the UK before moving to the UK. The money retains its tax-free nature, provided it is segregated from any future income or gains arising once the individual becomes UK resident.

It should be noted that gains realised after an individual becomes UK resident are calculated by reference to the cost of the asset when it was originally acquired, which may have been many years ago. There is no automatic uplift in the base cost to the market value of the asset at the date of UK arrival.

Consequently, there is a one-off opportunity for an individual to create clean capital by realising foreign gains before becoming UK resident. Care should be taken with the potential tax liability in the jurisdiction where an individual is tax resident when they make the gains. Owning an asset before becoming UK resident does not mean that the disposal proceeds can be remitted as clean capital, if it is sold after UK residence starts.

Establishing the correct date of arrival under the Statutory Residence Test is also fundamental to any pre-arrival planning. If an individual becomes UK resident earlier than anticipated, then money which they might have regarded as clean capital may in fact not be clean capital. The residence rules should be considered in full, but broadly it should not be assumed that split year treatment will apply without careful consideration of the conditions set out in Cases 4 to 8. In addition, the automatic UK residence tests can render an individual UK resident in unexpected circumstances where, for example, their only home is in the UK.

Planning with clean capital

Assuming it is possible to identify funds representing clean capital, it is then necessary to ensure that this capital is managed effectively so that it does not become tainted by being mixed with foreign income or gains arising while the individual is UK tax resident.

Superficially, this sounds simple enough. However, in practice this requires an individual's overseas bank accounts to be structured and operated in a specific way. The complexity of the offshore banking arrangements will typically depend upon the particular investment requirements of the client, and their willingness (or ability) to bear the opportunity cost of funds not being invested.

In theory, if clean capital is kept separately in one bank account, tax-free remittances from that account are possible, provided the interest earned on that account is credited directly to another account. The remittance rules operate on tracing rather than accounting principles, such that holding several separate bank accounts at the same bank does not result in funds within those accounts becoming 'mixed' for UK tax purposes.

Unless an individual is prepared to set aside an amount of clean capital in a non-interest bearing account for their UK spending, the operation of at least two separate overseas accounts will be required, i.e. a capital account, together with an income account to which the interest should be paid directly.

Where an individual has a sum of clean capital and wishes to invest the principal to generate a return, while also having the option of remitting clean capital in the future, more elaborate account structuring is then required. Any income, including interest and dividends, can be paid directly to the income account as before. However, at least two further accounts should be added: a capital gains account, to receive the sale proceeds from gainful investment disposals; and a capital loss account to receive the sale proceeds from investments sold at a loss. A remittance to the UK from the capital loss account should be tax free. A remittance to the UK from the capital gains account would represent part capital gain and part original clean capital.

In practice, depending on investment policy, a fifth account might also be contemplated to receive 'deemed' income such as income arising in relation to 'deeply discounted' securities, securities within the Accrued Income Scheme and offshore funds that do not have reporting status with HMRC. However, this may be considered to be an unnecessary complication if the intention is to never remit from any accounts other than the capital account itself.

Alternatively, the clean capital could be used as collateral for a 'back-to-back' loan arrangement, whereby the loan monies are invested as the individual wishes without compromising the clean nature of the clean capital used as collateral. Even in this scenario, the operation of multiple bank accounts could still be desirable.

Regardless of complexity, it is vital that the bank understands how the accounts need to be operated; otherwise, capital can all too easily become tainted by mixing foreign income and gains arising after UK arrival. Any of the structures outlined above requires careful planning and execution. Merely designating an account as a 'capital account' does not make it so as a matter of course. The correct operation of that account is paramount.

Bank errors

It is prudent to provide the bank with express written instructions as to how the accounts should be funded, structured, and operated on an ongoing basis. Where an inadvertent taxable remittance arises as a result of the bank acting contrarily to express instructions given by an account holder, HMRC accept that the account holder and the bank may alter the transaction in line with the original instructions given. This practice is based on case law (*Duke of Roxburghe's Executors v CIR* 20 TC 711).

However, it is unclear how far HMRC might allow this principle to extend in practice. For example, if a bank error results in clean capital becoming tainted but there has been no inadvertent remittance, HMRC might not accept that the principles of *Roxburghe* apply. What is clear is that specific instructions must have been given by the account holder and the bank needs to have made a genuine error in following those instructions. Therefore, in the absence of express written instructions, the *Roxburghe* defence is unlikely to be helpful.

Consequences of a mixed fund

Any failure to observe the planning principles described above might mean that clean capital becomes commingled with taxable elements of foreign income or gains, resulting in a so-called 'mixed fund'. A mixed fund is an account containing capital and more than one type of income or gains from one or more tax years.

Once a mixed fund is created, the tax treatment of any future remittance from that account is determined by specific ordering rules which work overwhelmingly against the taxpayer. Effectively, a remittance from a mixed fund is deemed to represent any income in the account, in priority to capital gains, and capital gains in priority to clean capital. These specific ordering rules are set out in full under section 809Q, ITA 2007, but suffice it to say the intended outcome is that categories of income or gains taxable at higher marginal rates are deemed to be remitted in priority to those taxable at lower rates.

It is not possible to 'clean up' a mixed fund simply by transferring an amount equal to the income within it to another offshore account. Specific rules also apply to so-called offshore transfers (section 809R (4), ITA 2007) such that they are treated as containing a proportionate element of each kind of income, capital gains, and capital comprising the account balance immediately before the transfer.

The only way to rectify a mixed fund is to remit the offending amount of income or gain to the UK which, by definition, results in a tax charge. Depending on the value and quantity of the transactions involved, the creation of a mixed fund can be costly for the individual concerned.

Alternative options if a mixed fund is created

Unless the *Roxburghe* defence is in point (see above), the options are limited if an individual wishes to bring funds comprising a mixed fund to the UK without incurring a tax liability.

Prior to 4 August 2014, there was a widely used HMRC 'concession' which ostensibly permitted non-doms to borrow using offshore mixed funds as collateral and remit the borrowed money to the UK without incurring a tax liability. This was subject to certain conditions being met. Specifically, the loan needed to be on commercial terms and serviced by regular interest payments. Many advisers considered that there was no legal basis for HMRC's published view, but nevertheless many non-doms relied on it to fund their UK spending.

Without warning, HMRC announced a change of position and it is no longer possible to procure a tax-free remittance to the UK by using mixed funds as collateral without the risk of an HMRC challenge. However, HMRC have since published new guidance confirming that arrangements where loans were brought into or used in the UK before 4 August 2014 will not be caught by the change in position, although these grandfathered loan arrangements can still give rise to tax liabilities if foreign income or gains are used to pay the loan interest or repay the principal.

Business investment relief

Another option which might be considered by individuals with mixed funds who wish to invest in the UK is business investment relief (BIR). The detail of the relief is set out in section 809VA et seq, ITA 2007. The main benefit is that cash remittances to the UK qualifying for BIR are tax-free providing the necessary conditions are met. Where BIR applies, no tax liability arises even if the money brought to the UK represents foreign income or gains that would, under normal circumstances, become taxable on remittance.

A number of conditions must be met in order for BIR to apply. Notably, the investment must be in a private limited company that is an eligible trading company. To meet the trading requirement, the company cannot undertake a 'substantial' extent of non-trading activities. HMRC view substantial as more than 20 per cent. The trade must be carried out on a commercial basis with a view to profit. Although the company shares cannot be listed on a recognised stock exchange, this still enables non doms to invest in AIM shares which are, technically, quoted rather than listed.

No minimum investment is required to secure BIR, nor is there a requirement for the investor to have any involvement with the companies in which they invest. In fact, one of the requirements of BIR is that the investor must not derive an 'abnormal' benefit from the company. However, once the money has been transferred to the UK, it must be used to purchase the shares within 45 days. Similarly, when the shares are sold, the proceeds must either be taken abroad or reinvested (in another qualifying investment) within 45 days. If these time limits are not observed, then a tax charge can arise. In addition, a claim for BIR must be submitted to HMRC within a strict time limit.

Practical points

Isolating and preserving clean capital are essential undertakings for foreign domiciled individuals, but this is a task easier said than done. It is important to appreciate that clean capital has a very specific meaning, which may not always be understood fully by clients and their advisers. This is not helped by the fact that there are different, more forgiving, definitions of capital for accounting or investment management purposes.

Furthermore, once clean capital has been correctly identified, it is important that it is managed carefully to preserve its nature. It is not unusual for clients and financial advisers to have a mistaken perception of what represents clean capital and how it can be managed. Therefore, if a non-domiciled client informs you that they have set aside capital to cover their UK living expenses tax efficiently, or that they have only made remittance of capital during the tax year, it pays to view any such assertions with a certain amount of professional scepticism.

If appropriate questions are not asked early on in the process, taxable remittances might arise unnecessarily or, worse, over time money which could have been maintained as clean capital becomes irreversibly commingled with amounts of foreign income or gains.

In terms of UK tax reporting obligations, it is important that the nature of remittances made by clients is determined and disclosed correctly to HMRC. HMRC are becoming increasingly aware of offshore bank accounts and payments to the UK. Therefore, it is good practice to ensure that the necessary analysis has been undertaken before tax returns are completed to ensure that any taxable elements have been identified and duly reported. If remittances are tax free, then this analysis will be valuable in concluding any enquiries made by HMRC at a later date.

More generally, there is value in having a proper discussion with clients who are contemplating a move to the UK at the outset to determine their UK spending requirements. It is not uncommon for clients to underestimate their UK expenditure or indeed the length of time they will continue to live in the UK. Similarly, living costs may rise if a larger UK property is desirable or other costs such as school fees become relevant. Some contingency should be factored in for unforeseen circumstances where possible.

Chapter 5: International succession planning and conflicts of law

By Sarah Sarwar, associate at Druces LLP

International migration has increased markedly as a result of the rise of the global labour market, more affordable international transport, and more sophisticated communication technologies. As such, it is no longer uncommon to have clients who accumulate assets in multiple countries in their lifetime. This creates a special challenge as the need to protect family and personal wealth requires more care and planning than ever before.

For instance, a now common scenario presented to a private client lawyer providing succession advice is for their client to be domiciled in one country, resident in another, while holding bank accounts in various tax shelters and a holiday home in a third country.

It would appear that while many wealthy international families are setting up their 'base' and/or are increasing their level of investment in the UK, few appreciate the implications that this may have with regard to the succession of their estate.

Every case is different. It is vital when planning one's international estate to look at their worldwide assets as a whole.

Applicable law in England

The first issue is to establish which legal system will govern each part of an individual's assets. Under English law, it is generally the domicile of the individual which will govern which system of law is applicable to different classes of assets (referred to as moveable and immovable assets) in their estate.

As a general rule, gifts of moveable assets, such as cash,

stocks and shares, or household goods are governed by the law of the deceased's domicile at death ('lex domicilii').

Gifts of immoveable assets are generally governed by the law of the country in which the land is situated ('lex situs'), regardless of the deceased's domicile.

Accordingly, where a non-UK domiciled person dies owning assets situated in England, English law will govern the succession and administration of their immovable property situated in England, but the law of their foreign domicile will govern the devolution of their moveable assets.

Further, if they were to die without leaving a valid will (or a non-UK valid will), then the English rules on intestacy will apply to their immovable property in England and their moveable assets will pass in accordance with the rules of succession as provided by the law of their domicile.

The meaning of 'domicile'

Our domicile of origin is that of our father or mother depending upon whether or not they were married at the date of birth. This can be altered in adult years if we move from our country of domicile of origin to another with the fixed intention of remaining permanently in that new country. In this circumstance, we will acquire a domicile of choice within the new home country.

It should be noted that a person's domicile under general law may be different to their domicile for inheritance tax purposes. So, for instance, a person may be domiciled under general law in Saudi Arabia, but deemed UK domiciled for UK inheritance tax purposes because they have lived in the UK for 17 out of the last 20 tax years.

Applicable law in common law countries

Common law jurisdictions such as England and Wales generally allow complete freedom as to the devolution of assets. In theory, this means that the testator is able to leave their entire estate to whomever they wish. However, in practice, the position is far less clear cut.

Generally, common law jurisdictions have laws which provide that dependants for whom no, or insufficient, provision has been made by the testator may apply to court for a share of the estate but relief is at the discretion of the court. Significantly, the English legislation in this respect as set out in the Inheritance (Provision for Family and Dependants) Act 1975 only applies where the deceased died domiciled in England and Wales. This is the case even if the deceased left property that is otherwise subject to English succession law. This is an interesting point of law and one which is likely to affect many more estates in the future, given the increased tendency for people to reside in the UK for extensive periods of time.

Accordingly, while the estate of an English domiciliary living in France would be caught by the 1975 Act, a Russian living in London with a non-UK domicile status could leave his entire estate to his girlfriend, cutting out his wife, and she would have no recourse under the 1975 Act. With the increase in cross-border family mobility and ownership of assets, the issue of domicile is becoming increasingly important in 1975 Act claims.

It is arguable that the 1975 Act is a statutory provision that is ripe for reform and the ability to make a claim against an estate should be extended to estates where the deceased was non-domiciled but 'habitually resident' (i.e. living in the UK for a settled purpose as part of the regular order of their life) in the UK. However, this may be difficult to regulate as it would mean that the UK courts would have the power to make orders over overseas assets which may or may not be enforceable in the country concerned.

CASE STUDY

Agulian and Cyganik

In the case of *Agulian and Cyganik* (2006), a claim was made under the Inheritance (Provision for Family and Dependants) Act 1975. The deceased, a Mr Nathanael, was born in Cyprus in 1939 but had been resident in London for approximately 43 years up to his date of death. He spent time in London in the 1950s and 1960s and returned to Cyprus in 1972. He was, however, forced to leave Cyprus in 1974 after the Turkish invasion. He went on to establish a substantial business in London and was engaged to be married to a woman with whom he resided in London, when he died unexpectedly in 2003.

On appeal, despite the long period of residence in the UK, the court found that Mr Nathanael was domiciled in Cyprus at the date of his death. Accordingly, his fiancée's claim under the 1975 Act failed as the court had no jurisdiction to hear a 1975 Act claim against the estate of a foreign domiciled person.

It could not be proved that Mr Nathanael had ever formed the intention to live in England permanently or indefinitely. In other words, he had retained his domicile of origin and there was insufficient evidence that he had acquired a domicile of choice in London. Various factors influenced the court. Mr Nathanael's strong emotional ties to Cyprus were noted, including his circle of friends in London who were members of the Greek Cypriot community; he continued to talk in Greek and watch Cypriot television; he sent money back to his family in Cyprus and had business interests in Cyprus. He had spoken to his bank manager of his intention to retire to Cyprus.

Applicable law in civil law countries and beyond

Civil law jurisdictions such as Spain and France apply a different approach in that their rules on succession are based on the law of an individual's habitual residence or citizenship and that this single legal system will govern their worldwide assets. The approach assumes its own laws will govern the succession of an individual's worldwide estate, but nevertheless accepts that the English courts will apply English law to the succession of immovable property situated in England.

Generally, civil law jurisdictions have some form of forced heirship, where at least a share of property and other assets must be left to certain members of the immediate family, usually a child or spouse. For instance, in Italy, assets must be left to a spouse or children, or older relatives if this isn't an option.

Forced heirship rules may also apply if an individual is a domiciliary of a Muslim country where Sharia law applies automatically. Under the general rules of Sharia law, a testator may freely dispose of up to one third of their estate to non-heirs. Male heirs receive double the inheritance of a female heir in the same category.

One will or two?

Once consideration has been given to which law (or laws) of succession and administration will apply to the testator's estate, it is thereafter necessary to ascertain whether there are restrictions which will limit the testator's freedom to dispose of their assets. It can then be determined whether it is sensible to have one will dealing with their worldwide estate or separate wills in each principal jurisdiction where the testator owns assets.

For instance, as noted above, the succession to UK situated moveable assets will be governed by the law of the deceased's domicile. If the deceased is domiciled in a country which imposes a forced heirship regime, then the terms of a UK will in contradiction to that regime, even if validly executed, will not be upheld in the UK. In such circumstances, it may be sensible therefore for an individual who is not domiciled in England to limit their English law will to the immoveable assets situated here.

CASE STUDY

Sharia law

Take the following example: a Saudi Arabian domiciled man who had been living in England for 30 years asks his lawyers to draft a new will for him. They draft a standard

English-law worldwide will giving everything to his wife if she survives him. They advise him that it is tax efficient to prepare a will on this basis due to the inheritance tax spouse exemption and the transferability of the nil rate band.

The solicitors were unaware that sharia law applied, due to the clients domicile. Equally, they did not know that sharia law prevented a man giving everything to his wife if he also has children.

The English law was invalid in respect of all of the client's moveable assets. Further examination of the estate showed that the only real estate he owned was held via an offshore company. The result was that the client owned moveable assets and did not own any immoveable assets. Sharia law therefore applied to *his whole estate* and the English law will was essentially invalid.

In such cases as the one described above, an option would be for a person to make wills in each legal jurisdiction in which they have assets. This would help speed up the administration of an estate on death. If a person has one will dealing with their worldwide estate, it is usual for the will to be proved firstly in the country in the jurisdiction in which they were domiciled, and then in each separate jurisdiction. The administration may be delayed until the formalities have been dealt with in the country of domicile. However, it is important that multiple wills work properly together, are appropriately limited in scope, and do not by default revoke the others.

Brussels IV – Is it the answer?

Close to 450,000 cross-border successions occur in the EU every year with a total estimated value of more than €123 billion. There have been various attempts over the years within the EU to present a unified system for tackling the issue of cross-border succession planning. However, it has unsurprisingly been difficult to get past the issue of the inherent difficulty of unifying common law systems, which generally allow testamentary freedom with civil law systems and their forced heirship rules.

On 17 August 2015, the European Succession Regulation 650/2012 (known as the Brussels IV) came into force with the purpose of harmonising the succession of estates in the EU Member States. Essentially, Brussels IV states that it is the law in which the deceased was 'habitually resident' (which need not be an EU member state) that should apply on succession. Habitual residence is determined by reference to an overall assessment of the circumstances of the life of the deceased during the years preceding their death and at the time of their death, taking account of all relevant factual elements, in particular the duration and regularity of the deceased's presence in the state concerned and the conditions and reasons for that presence. It is possible for the testator to make a clearly documented express election contrary to their habitual residence and to choose for the governing law of where they are a national to apply.

There are 25 states which have signed up to Brussels IV. However, Ireland, Denmark, and the UK have opted out of Brussels IV. The main reason for the UK's opposition relates to provisions within Brussels IV to claw back previous lifetime gifts, which is a common feature of civil law systems. The UK was concerned that this would lead to significant uncertainty in relation to lifetime gifts.

However, UK nationals will still be affected by Brussels IV as they can elect (likely in a will) to use English law where they have assets located in a continental jurisdiction – for example, they may want to avoid the forced heirship provisions commonly found under civil law systems or rely on the UK concept of joint tenancy in relation to property ownership.

Accordingly, citizens of EU countries who have come to the UK to live and work will now need to give some thought as to how the new regulation may affect how their property would pass on their death, particularly if they could be regarded as habitually resident here.

CASE STUDY

Brussels IV

Take the following example: Charlotte is currently living in London but has moved around in the last few years, having purchased assets along the way. By way of background, she was born in Ireland to French parents. Her entire family subsequently moved to France. Charlotte attended university in France and thereafter moved to London where she met her husband and started a family. Accordingly, although Charlotte lives in London, she is domiciled, for English law purposes, in France and is an Irish national. She owns properties in London and Paris. Charlotte has advised that she would like to leave all of her estate on her death to her husband and then, following his death, to her children.

Taking each asset in turn:

- Charlotte's property in London – This property will pass in accordance with the succession rules under English law that, generally speaking, allow testamentary freedom. Accordingly, Charlotte will be able to leave her property in accordance with her wishes. Brussels IV does not change the position in any way.
- Charlotte's property in Paris – Under the old French succession rules, Charlotte's property would have passed under the French forced heirship rules. However, under the new succession rules, as Charlotte is habitually resident in England, Brussels IV should mean that she should be able to avoid French forced heirship entirely and achieve the testamentary freedom that will allow her to leave her French property in

accordance with how she would like it to pass. However, French lawyers may take the view that England and Wales make renvoi ('sending back') to the law of France, meaning that French forced heirship rules should apply to the French property. Accordingly, a better solution would be for Charlotte to own her property in France *with her husband* in a 'Regime de Communauté Universelle'. This will avoid the forced heirship provisions and will ensure that the French property passes to the survivor immediately on the first death.

In summary

Brussels IV will most certainly go some way towards ending the EU disparity of testamentary freedoms on succession. However, the fundamental differences in deeply embedded cultural rules of the succession laws across the EU will most certainly make this a challenging exercise.

Brussels IV provides an excellent opportunity for those with multi-jurisdictional assets to take control of their heirs' financial future. At the core of succession planning is preservation of wealth and the introduction of an EU succession law is a major step forward in providing certainty in will writing for all those with assets in the EU.

Chapter 6: **Farmland succession**

By Julie Butler, managing partner at Butler and Co

With most landowning farmers in the UK aged in their 70–90s, there are often serious concerns over whether effective succession planning is in place. There are many reasons why farmers and landowners do not consider succession strategy. At a basic level, good succession needs a farming partnership agreement and all the partners must have wills. Examples of why farmers do not embrace succession planning include:

1) Worries over the cost of proper advice;
2) The farmers/landowners have to face the underlying conflicts and concerns over fairness between family members;
3) The farmers/landowners do not realise how all the current changes to land diversification put the inheritance (IHT) reliefs at risk on not just the farmhouse (agricultural property relief – APR), but also on other areas of the farm (business property relief – BPR); and
4) The misguided assumption that all farms escape 'death duties' regardless of planning.

Let's look first at the tax reliefs that have to be considered as part of succession planning.

Business property relief (BPR) and hope value

The primary intention of business property relief (BPR) is to enable businesses to cope with a death in the family or another inheritance tax (IHT) event without causing the entity to have to be sold. BPR is meant to be a 'relief'. It is important that BPR is considered in addition to agricultural property relief (APR), as the latter only covers the agricultural value of land and not the 'hope value' (the difference between agricultural value and market value). BPR instead covers the whole market value of the land, including any development potential inflating the value. So, the next important question that has to be asked is: does the current business structure protect BPR?

Farms present large succession concerns with regard to trying to achieve a balance between farmers within the family, but also to make sure the farm is not 'divided' into uncommercial units, i.e. to try to prevent fragmentational division. Development potential can be one solution to succession planning, i.e. the non-farming siblings can be paid development monies. It is therefore essential that maximum IHT reliefs and CGT reliefs are achieved on any development opportunities.

If only APR is claimed by the farming family, there may still be a significant IHT liability arising on non-farming assets, whereas a BPR claim would eradicate this extra liability entirely. In general terms, therefore, provided the potential development land is part of a trade and the trading tests (IHTA 1984 section 105(3)) are met, BPR should be achieved. If there are too many investments in the farming operation to qualify for BPR, then a withdrawal of these assets should be considered. The whole issue of the trading operation and the 'investment line' must be reviewed to ensure future IHT liabilities are minimised to achieve effective succession planning.

A large number of farming activities are deemed to be 'investment activities' and HMRC is pushing to define a large amount of diversification as 'investments' in order to collect more IHT.

Too many investment activities

Many farming operations have too many 'investment activities' making qualification for BPR uncertain, with potentially catastrophic tax consequences. Imagine the succession problems in the landmark case of *Balfour (Brander (representative of Fourth Earl of Balfour) v HMRC* [2010] STC 2666) if the claim for BPR on the mixed agricultural estate had failed. As a result of concerns of a '*Balfour* failure', i.e. where the operation is deemed to be mostly holding of investments, tests need to be carried out to check the trading element and this is why many farmers and landowners conduct the exercise known as 'the *Balfour* matrix'. Such an exercise looks at the business structure, income, profits, hours spent, and capital values over a period. The aim is to identify too many investments (a '*Balfour* failure'), i.e. to confirm trading has not passed the 'investment line' while the farmer/landowner is still alive as a protection for tax relief and succession planning.

Areas that HMRC define as 'investments' are the letting operation of cottages, workshops, industrial units, and solar parks. Furnished holiday accommodation has been attacked as an investment activity through the recent tribunal cases of *Pawson* and *Green*.

Another area of activity that HMRC is targeting as not qualifying for BPR is the trade of providing horse liveries where licences are given to customers with horses on their land. For farmers/landowners involved in this area of equine trade, it is well known that such an activity is very hard work and an 'intelligent businessman' would see this as a trading operation. Various matters must be looked at in order to evidence the claim for BPR, i.e. it is essential that trading accounts are prepared and that a high degree of services are provided.

Part of the solution to succession and tax concerns over the operation involving too many investments is to consider lifetime transfers to the next generation. Tax planning is not the only reason for farmers and landowners to consider lifetime transfers; there is also the legal protection of ensuring everything is passed down as it should be while the farmer is still alive.

Mental capacity and lifetime transfers

One problem of succession planning is that the next generation can enthusiastically encourage the passing down of the farm when the farmer is not yet ready to see this through. Some children who stay working on the farm consider the passing down of the farm as their 'right' for working so hard on the farm and they can encourage a lifetime transfer, possibly by exerting what is known as 'undue influence'.

There will therefore be the same professional protection needed around the lifetime transfer of the farm as to the mental capacity of the testator of a will, i.e. someone who is leaving the asset on death. For example, gifts made by ageing farmers who are possibly losing capacity need close scrutiny. Any tax adviser working in connection with tax planning around lifetime gifts, should work with a solicitor who will have similar responsibilities with regard to the drafting of the will, in deciding mental capacity on lifetime gifts.

If there are doubts for the tax adviser about the farming client's capacity, this may cause uncertainty and expense after the client's death, if the matter is not clarified at the time of the transfer. Complicated issues of judgement can arise for all those professional advisers involved in lifetime transfers, and protection needs to be considered from every angle. With farmland values at such a high level and so many development opportunities available, the quantum of risk has increased dramatically over the last few years.

While suggestions to clients about protection regarding capacity might be considered difficult or tactless, they need to be pursued. Tax planning around lifetime gifts is complex. The immediate impact of potential IHT and CGT liabilities have to be considered as part of all succession planning.

Capital gains tax (CGT) and inheritance tax (IHT) planning together

With many farmers wishing to pass farms down now, advisers must look at the tax position of a lifetime transfer for CGT and IHT together; each tax cannot be looked at in isolation. A lifetime gift of assets is still an effective sale for CGT purposes, and it has to be recorded as such. It could well be that a 'holdover election' is made for CGT purposes, where the farm qualifies for holdover relief, i.e. where the capital gain is 'held' over. The beneficiary will have to consider the loss of the 'tax-free uplift on death' on such a gift, i.e. they are taking on the base cost of the donor/transferor.

As mentioned, the most obvious tax planning route with regard to a lifetime transfer would be a holdover election as the farm is a business asset so that there is no CGT to pay on the transfer. The disadvantage is that the beneficiary will have the same base cost for CGT as the donor. The mechanics are that immediate CGT liability in a lifetime transfer can often be removed by a holdover election under TCGA 1992, section 165, where the transferee takes on the transferor's base cost. 'Base cost' can be interpreted as the tax cost of an asset to the owner.

What the family plans to use the farm for in the future has to be considered. If the children plan to stay at the farm a long time into the future, generally until death, the base cost will not be so key for CGT as there will not be a sale against which to match the base cost. However, should the children plan to sell the farm at some time in the future, they will be disadvantaged by the low tax base cost. If the farm was bought in, say, the 1970s a March 1982 value is used as the base cost. The holdover relief is, as set out, most often used in succession planning on passing on business assets to the next generation without any immediate CGT charge.

To present the matter bluntly 'death is not a chargeable event' so the CGT liability will only arise on sale. It will be important to ensure that all lifetime gifts are correctly recorded in the farm accounts. There are arguments to say that the correct valuation in the accounts is the market value at the date of transfer, although it has been passed over at cost. The accounts and the 'base cost control' will have to be updated for the change in ownership. The control is simply a way of recording how the farm's base cost develops over time through transfer on death, improvements, lifetime transfers, and the like. This will need to be reconciled with business accounts as applicable and a careful review of the relevant allocation of improvements will be essential.

The risks of the grazing agreement and CFA

Many landowners who are entering old age are often persuaded by land agents to move from 'in hand' farming to a grazing agreement or a contract farming arrangement (a CFA). Such a move can have a negative tax impact for tax efficient succession planning.

The landowner who wishes to secure CGT and IHT advantages for a trading activity must pay scrupulous attention to the nature of the grazing agreement and the activities he contracts to perform in association with it. The establishment of a trade also applies to a CFA. The statutory definition of 'farming' for both income tax and corporation tax purposes requires that, for the landowner of grass lands to be 'farming', he must show he is in occupation of the pasture and that this is for the purposes of husbandry. Because all farming is treated as the carrying on of a trade (ITTOIA 2005, section 9(1) and CTA 2009, section 36(1)), a landowner who establishes that they are farming land is treated as carrying on a trade with the land as a capital asset employed in it.

With increased land prices, the risks of using the grazing agreement and the CFA as a 'tool of tax protection' has become significant both with regard to APR on the farmhouse and BPR on potential development land. The essentials to ensure tax protection are a well-drafted legal document, and an understanding of what is really happening on the land and whether this counts as a trade in the 'eyes' of HMRC.

Scottish legal rights (forced heirship rules) and lifetime transfers

The consideration of farmland succession is particularly important at present in Scotland, where 'heirship rights' are different to the rest of the UK. 'Legal rights' are legally guaranteed powers available to a legal entity in realisation or defence of its just and lawful claims or interest. In the terms of succession, 'legal rights' are where children have a legal right to their parents' estates. Testamentary provisions are where parents make a will which overrides the legal rights of children in accordance with Scottish Law (guidance is given in IHTM 12229).

Legal rights can be claimed by the surviving spouse and the children of the deceased. The right to claim is automatic, no application to the court is necessary. The legal right of the surviving spouse is one third or one half of the net moveable estate depending on whether there are surviving children. Such rules have a massive impact on succession planning.

Legal rights have been a distinctive feature of Scottish Law for a very long time. Provided the prospective beneficiaries (spouse or children) survive the deceased's death, then they cannot lose their legal rights by any provision in the deceased's will. Testamentary provisions can only take effect after the legal rights have been met.

Legal rights only apply to 'moveable property' – currently farms are exempt from such qualification. A large number of farms traditionally are left to the farming children, i.e. those who have stayed farming, as a thank you for this loyalty and in an attempt to pass the farm intact down the generations. Such gifting to the farming children was traditionally to the eldest son, but this did ensure that the farm carried on without division.

Scottish consultation

Scottish farms have been exempt from legal rights which means farms can be passed down to the 'farming children' and not all the children equally. On 29 June 2015, the Scottish Government issued a consultation paper on the law of succession. Suggestions are that legal rights be abolished and replaced with legal share. In the 2009 report, the Scottish Law Commission concluded that there should no longer be an exemption for agricultural property.

Part of the suggestion of the consultation is that the farms and estates will no longer be exempt as qualifying as 'moveable property', but there will be some limited form of exemption from legal rights. The result would be fragmentation, subdivision, or sale. With careful planning, legal rights can be mitigated substantially if this is required. (Guidance is found at IHTM 12221 and IHTM 12227.)

Lifetime transfer and Scottish legal rights

As mentioned, forced heirship is a legal system which does not recognise the total freedom of testation. The forced estate is divided into shares which include the share of issue and the spousal share. The free estate, on the other hand, is at the discretion of a testator to be distributed by will on death to whomever they choose. Takers in the forced estate are known as 'forced heirs'.

One form of mitigation to the proposed changes to legal rights is lifetime transfer of the farm to the farming children now as an alternative to the fragmentation that could result from the Scottish legal rights consultation should it become law. This article has already looked at some of the complications in this regard. Such an action is in tune with many other UK farmers who are seeking to take advantage of the currently favourable tax reliefs. Consideration will obviously have to be given to the tax problems of lifetime transfers of the farms and estates so that the forced 'heirship rules' do not adversely impact on farms passing down the generations.

Action points

At a practical level, it is key for all farming families to discuss and consider succession, and for this to be supported by well-drafted legal agreements and evidence that supports those agreements. Where there are no legal agreements, evidence for tax relief and succession has to be obtained from other documents, for example this can be in the form of the tax return and accounts. In these circumstances, it is important to review all land and property page entries to ensure that the correct disclosure has been made in respect of the land. The tax return is part of the evidence to support claims for IHT and CGT and the preparation time is the ideal moment for the interactive 'fact find' to ensure tax protection.

The ultimate protection for succession planning is for the farming family to take proper tax and legal advice, to talk amongst themselves as to what they really want and also what will work practically moving forward, and how the tax planning protection can work. With current values, the tax protection *must* be in place as otherwise the farm could be lost to 'death duties' and 'dispute'.

As mentioned, it is imperative that legal agreements are in place to give legal clarity and to try to protect against family disagreements. The recent legal cases of *Davies*[1] (where there was a dispute over an unwritten partnership agreement) and *Ham*[2] (where the partnership agreement in place was inadequate) are practical guides for the need to sort out succession with good advice and strong legal agreements before the conflict becomes court action.

References

1. *Davies & Another v Davies* [2014] EWCA Civ 568.
2. *Ham v Ham* [2013] EWCA Civ 1301.

Chapter 7: What impact does *Ilott v Mitson* have on 1975 Act claims?

By Edward Hewitt, barrister at 3 Stone Buildings

Mrs Ilott's quest for reasonable financial provision from the £486,000 estate which her late mother left to animal charities in order to disinherit her has resulted in five separate court decisions, including two from the Court of Appeal, which have been widely reported – and criticised – in the media as landmark decisions which significantly undermine freedom of testamentary disposition and make it impossible for an individual to deliberately disinherit an adult child from whom they are estranged. This article asks what impact the *Ilott* litigation is likely to have on future claims brought pursuant to the Inheritance (Provision for Family and Dependants) Act 1975 ('the 1975 Act').

The facts

Melita Jackson married in 1956. In June 1960, her husband was killed in an accident at work while Mrs Jackson was pregnant. Their only child, Heather, was born three months later. Mrs Jackson received substantial compensation from her husband's employer, which she used to pay off the mortgage on her home. She then formed a relationship with another man with whom she had no further children, and with whom she raised Heather. He predeceased Mrs Jackson in 1996.

In 1978 Heather, who was then 17, left home during the night without her mother's knowledge to go to live with her young boyfriend, Nicholas Ilott, at his parents' house. Mrs Jackson strongly disapproved of Mr Ilott and did not want Heather to have anything to do with him. She reported her daughter as missing to the police, who found her at the Ilott family home, safe and well but refusing to return home. There was no contact between mother and daughter for the following five years.

Heather and Mr Ilott married in April 1983. Mrs Jackson was not invited to or informed of the wedding. Mr and Mrs Ilott went on to have five children together. Throughout their married life they lived in straightened financial circumstances in a three-bedroom house they rented from a housing association in a village in Hertfordshire.

Since Mrs Ilott had left home, she and Mrs Jackson had become estranged. Over the years there were three attempts at reconciliation, all of which ultimately failed.

In 2002 Mrs Jackson made a will by which she left a legacy of £5,000 to the BBC Benevolent Fund and the rest of her estate to be divided between The Blue Cross, the Royal Society for the Protection of Birds, and the Royal Society for the Prevention of Cruelty to Animals. The evidence indicated that during her life she had had no particular interest in birds or animals or in any of the charities.

With her will, Mrs Jackson left a letter in which she explained the reasons why she had chosen to disinherit her daughter. At the same time, she wrote to Mrs Ilott explaining her decision to disinherit her. Mrs Ilott replied that she was very upset by her mother's rejection and suggesting that Mrs Jackson might nevertheless have wished to make some provision for her grandchildren.

Mother and daughter had been estranged for some 26 years when Mrs Jackson died aged 70 on 10 July 2004, leaving an estate worth £486,000.

The litigation

After her mother's death, Mrs Ilott brought a claim against her estate seeking reasonable financial provision pursuant to the 1975 Act. In the summer of 2007, the first instance judge in the County Court held that Mrs Jackson had acted in an unreasonable, capricious, and harsh way towards Mrs Ilott, but that both sides were responsible for the failure of the attempts at reconciliation. The judge concluded that the will failed to make reasonable financial provision for Mrs Ilott and awarded her a lump sum of £50,000.

Mrs Ilott appealed against the quantum of the trial judge's order. As a result the charities cross-appealed arguing that he had failed to properly apply the law and that he should have held that it had been reasonable in all the circumstances for Mrs Jackson to make no provision at all for Mrs Ilott and should have dismissed her claim. After some delay, the appeal and cross-appeal came before Eleanor King J (sitting in the Family Division as an appellate court) who, as a result of time constraints, was invited to give judgment on the charities' cross-appeal first.

In a judgment handed down on 1 December 2009,[1] Eleanor King J held that the trial judge had erred in law by focusing too heavily on the rights and wrongs of the attempts at reconciliation and had asked himself the wrong question, i.e. whether Mrs Jackson had acted unreasonably in disinheriting Mrs Ilott, instead of asking himself 'whether on an objective basis, having considered all the factors in section 3, the resulting provision, or lack of it, is unreasonable'. Moreover, he had erred in his balancing of the section 3 factors 'with the consequence that he was plainly wrong in concluding that the deceased had failed to make reasonable financial provision for the daughter'. She therefore allowed the charities' cross-appeal and dismissed Mrs Ilott's claim.

In March 2011, the Court of Appeal unanimously allowed Mrs Ilott's appeal against Eleanor King J's decision.[2] The court held that the trial judge had asked himself the right question and had conducted the section 3 exercise correctly, and that Eleanor King J had therefore been wrong to overturn his decision. Having allowed Mrs Ilott's appeal, the court directed her appeal against quantum to be listed before a judge other than Eleanor King J.

After some further delay, Mrs Ilott's appeal against quantum was heard by Parker J, who dismissed it in March 2014.[3]

However, in July 2015, the Court of Appeal allowed Mrs Ilott's appeal against Parker J's decision,[4] holding that the trial judge had made two 'fundamental errors of law':

'First… DJ Million states that because of the appellant's lack of expectancy and her ability to live within her means, her award should be "limited". In the paragraphs which follow he does not state how he has limited the award to reflect those matters.… Those matters might justify a less generous award than would otherwise be made, but, even if that was so, it was wrong in law to state that the award had been limited for those reasons without explaining what the award might otherwise have been and to what extent it was limited by the matters in question. It was a situation in which reasons were required so that the appellant could consider whether the reductions were excessive (which might give her an arguable error for the purposes of any appeal), and it is of the essence of a judicial decision that adequate reasons are given on material matters…

The second fundamental error in my judgment is this. The judge was required to calculate financial provision for the appellant's maintenance. Yet he did not know what effect the award of £50,000 would have on her state benefits. He made a working assumption… that the effect of a "large capital payment" (which would include an award such as he ultimately made) would disentitle the family to most if not all of their state benefits. Failure to verify this assumption undermined the logic of the award.'

As a result, the court set aside the trial judge's decision, re-exercised the statutory powers itself, and awarded Mrs Ilott a lump sum of £143,000 plus expenses to enable her to exercise her right to buy her home from the housing association together with a further optional lump sum of up to £20,000 'to provide an immediate capital sum from which further income needs can be met', structuring the award in that way so as to preserve Mrs Ilott's state benefits. At the time of writing, it is unclear whether the charities will try to appeal to the Supreme Court.

Impact

Several questions have been asked in both the popular and the legal press in the aftermath of *Ilott*. Some of these are relevant to the non-contentious will draftsman whose client is likely to want to do whatever they can to pre-empt a 1975 Act claim being brought after their death. Others are relevant to the litigator whose client will want to know what the prospects are of successfully bringing or defending a 1975 Act claim, and thus what the court's approach is likely to be. What follows provides some suggested answers to some of these questions.

For the non-contentious practitioner

'Is there any point in making a will if a judge can, in effect, re-write it after the testator has died?'

It is suggested that the answer is a resounding 'yes'. A straightforward way of demonstrating this is to point out that in *Ilott* itself, had Mrs Jackson not made a will at all and died intestate, her daughter would have inherited the whole estate, which was (rightly or wrongly) the precise opposite of what Mrs Jackson intended. Moreover, there are all sorts of other reasons why an individual may prefer to make a will instead of letting the intestacy rules determine how their estate will pass on death. The testator may wish to appoint particular individuals to act as their executors and/or as guardians to any minor children; they may wish to leave particular items of great sentimental value (such as items of furniture, jewellery, photographs, paintings) to particular individuals. Finally, as discussed further below, the testator's intentions as implemented in their will, and any explanation given for such intentions, are one of the factors the court is likely to take into account when carrying out the section 3 exercise.

It is suggested that none of this has been affected by the decisions in *Ilott*. Contrary to some of the suggestions made in the popular press, what undermines freedom of testamentary disposition is the 1975 Act itself, not the *Ilott* litigation. This is nothing new: the 1975 Act has been in force for 41 years and its predecessor (the Inheritance (Family Provision) Act 1938) was on the statute book for 37 years before that.

'I want to disinherit X, but I am concerned that X will then bring a 1975 Act claim against my estate. What can I do to prevent this?'

The starting point is that it is not possible to oust the jurisdiction of the court altogether and therefore to preclude X from bringing a 1975 Act claim in a fool-proof way.[5] This was the case before *Ilott* and remains the position after it.

On the other hand, various steps can be taken to try to minimise the risk of X bringing a claim and of such a claim succeeding. Which steps are likely to be most effective will depend on the particular circumstances. In general terms, it will be helpful for the testator to explain the reasons why he wishes to disinherit X and for such an explanation to be recorded in detail in the will itself, in an accompanying letter, and/or in the attendance note which records the testator's instructions, as this is one of the factors the court will take into account when carrying out the section 3 exercise. Depending on the circumstances, some thought should also be given as to whether it may be better for the testator to leave something to X rather than nothing at all in order to make a 1975 Act claim by X more difficult. It is suggested that *Ilott* has not changed the effectiveness of these steps, as illustrated by the fact that, in all five decisions, the court took into account and gave weight to Mrs Jackson's clear intention to disinherit her daughter.

'If I want to disinherit X, should I leave my estate to charity instead?'

This is perhaps the most controversial – and, it is suggested, unintended – consequence of the most recent decision in *Ilott*. The Court of Appeal pointed out that Mrs Jackson had no particular connection with the charities to whom she had left her estate under her will and suggested that, as a result, the charities could have no expectation to benefit from Mrs Jackson's estate (as contrasted with Mrs Ilott who, as Mrs Jackson's only daughter, could). While no single factor is ever decisive, the judgment suggests that this factor weighed in favour of Mrs Ilott's claim (or at least did not weigh against it). Moreover, the Court of Appeal noted that it was common ground that the charities had no competing financial need which might weigh against Mrs Ilott's claim pursuant to section 3(1)(c).

The result of all this appears to be that a testator who strongly wishes to disinherit X and to do whatever they can to ensure X will not be able to bring a successful 1975 Act claim against their estate may well be advised to leave the estate to an individual who is in financial need (such as a relative, a friend, or a neighbour), and preferably one for whom the testator is already financially responsible, rather than to charity because if X later brings a 1975 Act claim the individual beneficiary will be able to show competing financial need and competing expectation, whereas a charity will not.

The position may be different if the testator has a connection with a particular charity (e.g. because he regularly donates to it or fundraises for it and/or is involved in its management) and/or a particular interest in a charity's activity (e.g. in a charity which furthers research to find a cure for an illness from which the testator is suffering or which was responsible for the death of one of the testator's relatives, or in a charity which furthers an art form about which the testator is passionate). In such cases, the connection and the reasons why the testator wishes to make provision for the charity in question (as well as the reasons why the testator wishes to disinherit X) should be carefully recorded in detail.

Impact for the litigator

'Does the Ilott *litigation make it easier for claims brought by adult children to succeed?'*

It is suggested that the answer is 'no' and that none of the decisions in *Ilott* has changed the law or the court's approach to 1975 Act claims brought by adult children. Like all other 1975

Act claims, *Ilott* presented a unique combination of circumstances. Had any one of these been different, it is likely the outcome would have been different too.

The Court of Appeal had previously made it clear[7] that 1975 Act claims brought by adult children must be approached in the same way as any other 1975 Act claim, i.e. by an evaluation of all of the section 3 factors. In particular, no gloss should be imposed on the statute; and it is therefore not necessary for an adult child to establish, in addition to the section 3 factors, that the deceased owed them a 'moral obligation' or that there are other 'special circumstances' in order for the claim to succeed.[8]

As a general proposition, it seems fair to say that an adult child who is financially independent is likely to face an uphill struggle in bringing a successful 1975 Act claim when all of the section 3 factors are considered, but of course it all depends on the particular circumstances. The various decisions in *Ilott* simply reiterate and confirm this.

'How will the court treat the fact that the estate has been left to charity rather than to a relative?'

The short answer is, of course, 'it depends'. However, as explained above, *Ilott* appears to indicate that charities do not have a competing financial need (for the purposes of section 3(1)(c)), and that whether a charity is able to argue that it has a competing expectation is likely to depend on whether the testator had any particular connection to or interest in the charity in question.

'How will the court treat the fact that the claimant is on state benefits?'

The various decisions in *Ilott* seem consistent in treating Mrs Ilott's future entitlement to state benefits as part of her financial resources to be taken into account pursuant to section 3(1)(a) and in seeking to structure any award so as to preserve such entitlement. Sir Nicholas Wall P explained that 'although [Mrs Ilott's] current income is largely made up of benefits and tax credits, I do not base my decision on the ground that a claim under the Act can properly be used to relieve the State of the obligation to support an applicant'.[9] In its second decision, the Court of Appeal expressly held that 'this is a case where the court can and should make reasonable financial provision out of the deceased's estate for [Mrs Ilott's] maintenance so that her living expenses are relieved without affecting the state benefits on which she relies'.[10]

References

1. [2009] EWHC 3114 (Fam)).
2. [2011] EWCA Civ 346.
3. [2014] EWHC 542 (Fam).
4. [2015] EWCA Civ 797.
5. Unless, perhaps, X is the testator's ex-spouse, in which case the divorce court should be asked in the context of the divorce proceedings to make an order pursuant to section 15 of the Act preventing either party from making a 1975 Act claim against the estate of the other.
6. [2015] EWCA Civ at [51](iv). See also e.g. *Christofides v Seddon* [2014] WTLR 215 at [89]).
7. See e.g. *Re Coventry* [1980] Ch 461 at 486F-G; *Re Hancock* [1998] 2 FLR 346 at [13]; *Espinosa v Bourke* [1999] 1 FLR 74.
8. Which appeared to have been suggested at first instances in *Re Coventry* [1980] Ch 461 at 486F-G, although the Court of Appeal in *Re Coventry* itself made it clear that that was not in fact the case: 'Oliver J. nowhere said that a moral obligation was a prerequisite of an application under section 1(1)(c); nor did he mean any such thing' ([1980] Ch 461 at 486F-G, *per* Goff LJ).
9. [2011] EWCA Civ 346 at [14].
10. [2015] EWCA Civ 797 at [67].

Chapter 8:
A question of trusts – Types of trust and their role in tax and succession planning

By Anna Coakes, senior associate, and John FitzGerald, solicitor, at Gordon Dadds

There is a long-standing perception that high net worth individuals establish trusts purely as a means of avoiding tax, specifically inheritance tax. While the use of trust structures can, in very limited circumstances, help to mitigate inheritance tax, government legislation has now largely eroded the privileged tax status of most trusts. At the same time, the regulatory and compliance obligations imposed on such structures are, these days, substantial. It is therefore important, when asked to advise a client about settling assets into a trust, for the solicitor to consider the client's primary motivation for the use of a trust or trusts, and whether a trust is necessarily the best means of achieving their client's ends.

Although the heyday of trusts may now have passed, there nonetheless remain numerous circumstances in which the options and benefits provided by trusts are highly advantageous and where the use of such a structure may still be beneficial and justifiable, despite any adverse tax treatment. This article outlines the main situations where trusts continue to play an important role in succession planning.

Choosing the trust

It is possible for assets to be settled into trust either during the settlor's lifetime or upon the death of the settlor, according to the terms of the will. In both cases, it is possible for assets to be added to pre-existing settlements, although this may have tax consequences. Two of the main trust structures employed by settlors are discretionary trusts and interest in possession trusts.

Interest in possession trusts usually (but not always) take the form of an interest for life, where the beneficiary (known as the life tenant) is entitled during their lifetime to the income derived from the trust assets, but not to the underlying capital itself. Upon the death of the life tenant, the capital passes according to the terms of the trust, rather than the will of the life tenant or the provisions of the intestacy legislation.

The benefit of this structure, and the main reason that it is utilised, is that the settlor is able to control the ultimate destination of the settled assets. It is often used by settlors to ensure that, on death, their spouse receives the income from their estate and the capital passes to their children on the death of their spouse.

This option is particularly attractive should the settlor fear that their spouse may remarry subsequent to their death and their estate may be redirected to individuals whom they would not wish to inherit some or all of their estate. It is also increasingly common nowadays for settlors to have children from previous marriages and/or step-children, and the interest in possession structure enables the settlor to benefit their current spouse while safeguarding their own children's inheritance for the future.

It is possible for the trustees to use their discretion to advance capital to the life tenant if it should be necessary, and in cases where the trust assets include residential property, it is possible for the trust document to include provision for the life tenant to live in the property during the term of the trust, and for the same terms to apply to any subsequent property if the life tenant wishes to downsize.

An interest in possession may also be used to delay the date at which the beneficiary becomes entitled to the trust capital. This may be desired where the settlor has concerns about the maturity (or lack thereof) of the beneficiary. In such a case, the settlor may be worried that if the beneficiary receives the capital at too young an age they may squander the capital, and so the settlor may wish for the beneficiary only to be able to access the capital at an age where they would be sensible in respect of the capital windfall.

In some circumstances, the settlor may wish for a greater degree of flexibility and a discretionary trust may be more appropriate. This requires that there be more than one beneficiary and no beneficiary has a present right to enjoyment of the income, nor indeed of the capital. The trustees have absolute discretion as to whom receives what and when, although they must comply with their fiduciary duties in exercising this discretion.

A correctly drafted discretionary trust should afford sufficient flexibility for wealth to be protected through several generations of extended family. It also allows decisions about distributions, whether of income or capital, to be made at an appropriate time, rather than predicted many years in advance (as might be the case of a gift otherwise left under the terms of a will). It allows the trustees to make such decisions in light of the beneficiaries' circumstances at the date of the distribution, rather than the date of the settlement.

This is relevant in the case of younger beneficiaries, but especially those that might be considered to be (or to become) 'wayward'. The client may also be concerned about the dilution of family wealth if assets are left to beneficiaries outright, in particular if there is a question of those assets being drawn into a division of property on marital breakdown. The use of trusts in such circumstances will provide some protection, but care should be taken to consider the timing of the transfer of assets into a trust.

Trusts and inheritance tax

The incidence of inheritance tax will be an important consideration for the client and may affect the form of trust structure or structures adopted. Following the Finance Act 2006, for inheritance tax purposes, most settlements including discretionary trusts will fall within the relevant property regime. The settlement of any assets above the nil rate band, currently £325,000, available to the settlor at the date of settlement will attract a charge to inheritance tax.

Transfers upon death will attract inheritance tax at the full death rate of 40 per cent, and those during life at half this rate at 20 per cent, although the full 40 per cent will become payable (subject to taper relief) if the settlor dies within seven years. While these charges are significant, it is worth noting that the same 40 per cent inheritance tax rate would apply regardless of whether or not the estate is settled into a trust structure upon death, unless the assets are settled into a special trust such as a charitable trust.

Where the value of trust assets settled exceeds the nil rate band, appointments of capital out of the trust to a beneficiary will give rise to an exit charge of somewhere between 0 per cent and 6 per cent of the value of appointed funds, and the trust will also be subject to a periodic charge of up to 6 per cent on every 10 year anniversary of the settlement.

For those clients who are attracted to the flexibility of a discretionary trust, the inheritance tax charging regime will not necessarily be off-putting. One of the main benefits is that, while the trust is subject to these exit and periodic charges, the death of a beneficiary does not trigger any inheritance tax charge.

This is in contrast to the tax treatment of many interest in possession trusts. As with the relevant property regime, the transfer into an interest in possession trust is a chargeable transfer for inheritance tax purposes, but under section 49 of the Inheritance Tax Act 1984, a person beneficially entitled to an interest in possession in settled property is treated as beneficially entitled to that property provided that, if that interest was created after 22 March 2006, it qualifies as an immediate post death interest. In order for this to be satisfied, the settlement must be effected by will (or intestacy), and the beneficiary must be entitled to the interest in possession immediately following the settlor's death.

Importantly, where a life interest is left upon death to a surviving spouse, it is still possible to make use of the spousal exemption, and in these circumstances, it is possible to mitigate inheritance tax entirely on the death of the first spouse.

Once the assets have been settled into the interest in possession trust, they are considered for inheritance tax purposes as assets of the life tenant or beneficiary and there are no charges to inheritance tax either for distributions or on anniversary dates. However, in the event that the beneficiary dies during the term of the trust, the settled assets will be aggregated with the beneficiary's free estate for inheritance tax purposes. It is, therefore, vital for careful consideration to be given to the objectives of the client in light of their specific circumstances.

Pilot trusts

Under the relevant property regime, exit and periodic charges are calculated with reference to the value of the trust either on the date of settlement (exit charges) or at the date of the 10 year anniversary (periodic charges). In both cases, however, they are calculated with reference to the settlor's nil rate band available at the date of settlement, taking account of the settlor's cumulative total of chargeable transfers within seven years prior to this date.

This anomaly gave rise to the widespread use of what is known as a 'pilot trust': a trust designed to be constituted with a nominal initial fund in order to facilitate later more substantial additions to the trust property. Commonly, a settlor would establish a number of separate discretionary trusts on different days (to ensure that they were not treated as 'related settlements' and, therefore, combined for the purposes of the inheritance tax calculations) with a small initial fund, such as £10.

This would mean that, for each separate pilot trust, almost the entirety of the settlor's nil rate band would be available. The settlor could then provide under the terms of their will for a sum equivalent to (or sometimes just below to take account of inflation) the nil rate band to be settled into each pilot trust. Inheritance tax was, of course, payable on the estate, but because of the size of the nil rate band available to each trust, the inheritance tax charges over the life of each pilot trust would be minimal or indeed nil.

Provisions brought in last year, however, as part of Finance Act (No. 2) 2015 finally sounded the death knell for such schemes. The same-day addition rules mean that when calculating the exit and periodic charges for a specific relevant property regime trust, the value of any other relevant property regime trusts into which funds have been transferred on the same day that funds have been transferred into the other trust is taken into account.

For the purposes of transfers upon death into various pilot trusts, this means that on the death of the settlor, the aggregated value of all the pilot trusts receiving funds under the will would be taken into account for the inheritance tax charges for each trust. This has effectively negated the inheritance tax savings of pilot trusts, but for a few specific ones such as protected trusts.

Nevertheless, it is also worth pointing out that the proposed 'settlement nil rate band' (SNRB) has now been abandoned by the government. This would have given a settlor a single nil rate band, in addition to their personal nil rate band, to be applied across the board to all relevant property regime trusts which the settlor had established at any stage during their lifetime. The fact that the SNRB has not been adopted means that a settlor can still use their personal nil rate band every seven years to create a new trust.

For example, a settlor could make a gift of £30,000 into a discretionary trust every seven years. Assuming the settlor has made no other gifts in the previous seven years, there will be no charge to inheritance tax as the gift would fall within their personal nil rate band. In each trust, periodic charges would only be payable in the event that the value of the assets increases above £325,000.

Interaction of trusts and divorce

As practitioners will be aware, the jurisdiction of the courts in relation to financial matters in divorce has a wide reach in England. That is not to say, however, that the court will seek to disturb a family trust established well in advance of a marriage, particularly if that involves multiple generations.

In the case of a successful entrepreneur or professional who acquires significant wealth during a marriage, who then creates a trust during the marriage, the English divorce court might be more willing to look behind the transfer of the assets into the trust lest that transfer be seen as an attempt to put the trust beyond the reach of the court.

In circumstances where assets are transferred into a discretionary trust during a settlor's lifetime, where the trustees are prone to listening to the wishes of the settlor concerning requests for distribution (rather than exercising their own discretion), the trust structure is likely to be 'looked through'. There is a danger that such assets will be treated as those of the settlor (for the purpose of determining the financial settlement on divorce) if they are still effectively within their control.

The practitioner should be cautious about advising settlors in such circumstances who are seeking to use a trust to put assets beyond the reach of a spouse in the event of the marriage breaking down. The practitioner would need to consider carefully the timing of the creation of the trust, and transfer of assets into it, the method of control or the extent to which the settlor appears to be exercising control, the intended beneficiaries, and the extent to which the settlor is aiming to use the trust to manipulate what might be available for a financial settlement.

The best prospect of preserving wealth within a trust created during marriage will result if it is able to be shown that, at the time the trust was created, it was done so with the genuine intention of benefitting future generations, and ideally with the active involvement and support of both spouses.

Trusts and insolvency

The practitioner should also consider the situation where a client is seeking to use a trust to defeat a potential claim in bankruptcy. Section 283 of the Insolvency Act 1986 provides that a bankrupt's estate comprises all property belonging to, or vested in, the bankrupt at the commencement of the bankruptcy. The only exception is exempt property, which includes property held by the bankrupt on trust for any other person.

As practitioners will be aware, the trustee in bankruptcy acts for the benefit of unsecured creditors and is under a duty to realise assets for the benefit of those creditors. In the course of administering the bankruptcy, the trustee will consider whether a trust is capable of being challenged to increase the assets which are available for the creditors.

The trustee in bankruptcy has far-reaching powers to challenge a trust. The timing of the creation of the trust will be of significant importance. If the trust was settled within the relevant period before the issuing of the bankruptcy petition, it is open to be challenged as a preferential transaction. The relevant period will be six months, although this is extended to two years if the transaction is with the associate of the bankrupt (see Section 340 of the Insolvency Act 1986).

A declaration of trust may also be considered to be a transaction defrauding creditors, whereby assets are intentionally put beyond the reach of creditors. The trustee may investigate the declaration and will also consider the timing of the trust as well as the genuine purpose and use. The trustee may also investigate whether the beneficiaries have knowledge of the trust and its intended purpose.

Conclusion

Despite the recent attacks on the tax avoidance nature of trusts and the complicated legislation that this has resulted in, trusts continue to be a vital tool for succession planning. What is important is that the practitioner is certain early on what are the client's true objectives and what they wish to achieve.

Trusts remain a powerful weapon not only for long-term tax planning, but more importantly as a means of protecting wealth through generations, whether that be ring-fencing funds from an acrimonious divorce or keeping the money out of the pockets of the prodigal son.

Chapter 9:
The recent pension reforms and further changes on the horizon

By Penny Cogher, partner at Irwin Mitchell LLP

April 2015 heralded the introduction of the start of some of the most significant pension reforms for nearly 100 years. The April 2015 pension freedoms mean just that: entrusting individuals with the use, in particular, of their defined contribution (DC) pension savings and giving them direct access to their pension savings from age 55 onwards.

Individuals are now allowed to take these monies as cash, as a one-off payment or as a series of payments, or to use them for more flexible income drawdowns, or to buy an annuity, or to choose a combination of all these. Additionally, many of the old restrictions on the form of the annuity which had to be purchased from pension monies have been lifted.

These freedoms are all subject to the appropriate tax being paid on the withdrawal or use of the pension monies by or for the individual. The basic principle still remains that 25 per cent can be paid out tax free, and the appropriate advice must be taken.

Passing pensions down the generations

With the new pension flexibilities, more can be done than purely saving for a pension. There is now the possibility of passing pension savings down through the generations. This can be done simply by withdrawing the savings as cash (less the tax) and then using the money in a different way. Alternatively, and more interestingly, individuals can use an income drawdown product where the pension savings in the product can be inherited by the next generation(s). However, it is still very much early days for this so it is difficult to assess how popular, and how well used, this option might become.

Certainly, as the lifetime allowance reduces from £1.25 million to £1 million from 6 April 2016, there will be less scope for this type of product as individuals are more likely to use their pension pot fully before they die, particularly if life expectancies continue to increase. It seems to be increasingly likely that this type of passing pension wealth down the generations is only of real interest and use to high- and ultra-high-net-worth individuals. That said, research by the Resolution Foundation shows that the recently retired enjoy a higher proportion of the national wealth than the under 45s, with those aged between 65–74 holding 19 per cent of the UK's wealth.[1]

How ready have the providers been for the changes?

One difficulty with implementing such sweeping reforms is that it has taken providers some considerable time to work out how to change their pension products to reflect the new pension freedoms. Even now, none of the providers have products which provide all of the new pension flexibilities. Perhaps it is not so surprising, given how complex some of the changes have proved to be and how many legacy pension products remain where it is too complex and/or costly for providers to rush ahead and change them.

One key issue the pension industry is still working through, for example, is how a DC fund's default fund should operate so far as life-styling is concerned, given that there are so many permutations as to how and when an individual should be able to access their pension savings. Interestingly, in January 2016, while providers were working to bring new products to market, 55 per cent of them cited legacy technology as being a major obstacle to doing so. For all industries, maintaining good quality and up-to-date technology is a challenge and the pension industry is no different.

What about the financial advisers?

Financial advisers are another part of the pension community that is still reeling from the implications of the new pension freedoms. There are strict rules on what pension access individuals can have before they need to take specific advice from a specialised independent financial advisor (IFA). The government has also, of course, set up Pension Wise to provide free, impartial information and guidance to enable consumers to make the correct decision for them, but this falls short of being advice.

Even though Pension Wise is a free service, the FCA's findings published on 7 January 2016 state that, of 178,990 consumers, only 17 per cent used Pension Wise.[2] This increased to 22 per cent of consumers with small pots where there is less use of (and less requirements for) regulated advice. It remains important, however, that individuals do take appropriate financial advice if they want to purchase an annuity. The average healthy 65 year old with a pension pot of £100,000 could miss out on 14.5 per cent of income if they fail to shop around.[3]

Insurers have been reluctant to implement pension requests without the individual first having IFA advice, even if legally such advice is not required. There has also been a shortage of appropriate qualified advisers to provide the advice, and those that are qualified have tended to charge higher amounts than the individuals are used to, or are willing to pay. Various solutions to this have been suggested, including using 'robo advice' to help fill the gap and/or extending Pension Wise so that it can provide more tailored guidance.

Have the other pension freedoms changed the UK's pension saving patterns?

In terms of boosting pension savings, the pension reforms and the way they interact with auto-enrolment appear to have been successful. The ONS figures for the third quarter of 2015 show, for example, a net investment of £33 billion by insurance companies, pension funds, and trusts – the highest level since the second quarter of 2009.[4] Additionally, the average pension pot, according to research published in January 2016, used to buy an annuity has increased from £22,000 to £42,000.[5]

This may partly be because more people who are accessing their pension monies now have been a member of a DC scheme for longer and so have had time to build up a larger pot. However, the AEGON UK Readiness Report also concludes that the pension freedoms have caused an uplift in pension savings, with 16 per cent saving more as a direct result of the reforms and the average pension contributions increasing from £204 to £450 per month. Not surprisingly, there is less awareness of these changes among the UK's youth. 20 per cent of those surveyed by MRM Young Money aged between 18–25 admitted they know nothing about pensions and do not save for their retirement.[6]

How engaged are investors?

Despite the increase in pension savings, mandatory financial advice, brokers' charges, and administration charges will reduce an individual's final pot considerably. I suspect this, more than anything else, has resulted in consumers remaining wary of the pensions industry, pension providers, and pension products. It is certainly still difficult for a consumer to determine for themselves whether their pension product represents good value, and if it is a good quality product overall. There continue to be pockets of society who are disengaged from pensions. Research from Share Centre says that, despite the recent pension reforms, 11 per cent of those surveyed are still relying on an inheritance to fund their retirement.[7]

What has been the impact on DB schemes?

The DC pension freedoms seem to have proved popular with members of defined benefit, final salary schemes, many of whom have to transfer their benefits out to DC arrangements before they can access their pension benefits flexibly. The number of transfers out from DB schemes doubled in October/November 2015 when compared to the number in January 2015, as shown by the Xafinity transfer value index.[8]

The pension reforms have resulted in some defined benefit schemes considering whether to change the actuarial factors used in the calculation of their transfer values to make transfers out more attractive to their members. Each transfer out which a defined benefit scheme administers reduces the scheme's overall pension liabilities, and so overall helps the scheme's sponsoring employer to manage its pension obligations. There was concern when the pension flexibilities were first introduced that they would result in a run on member requests for transfers out for defined benefit (DB) schemes, but this does not appear to have happened yet.

Is the system working?

Encouragingly, the Financial Ombudsman has stated that the new pension reforms have so far resulted in a relatively small number of enquiries and complaints, although this does seem to go against the number of pension scams that have been publicised. According to the RSM Pension Fraud Risk Report, one third of pension schemes experienced some kind of fraud in 2015 – more than double the number in 2013.[9] Probably, it is still too soon to determine how successful the reforms have been in practice from this perspective, given the long-term impact the way in which an individual accesses their pension savings will have on that individual – there are likely to be repercussions for many years into the future.

Significant further changes for April 2016

Going forward, the whole pensions industry is waiting to find out what further changes, due in April 2016, the treasury might make to the whole system of tax relief on pension savings. The proposals are for either a single rate of tax relief for pension contributions (say 33 per cent), or to treat pensions like ISAs where contributions are subject to tax but withdrawals are not.

In the meantime, the industry is concerned about the impact of reducing the lifetime allowance to £1 million and tapering down the annual allowance for higher earners. The Pensions and Life Time Savings Association (formerly the NAPF) has even gone so far as to say that any move to end pension tax breaks for higher earners would effectively 'kill off' work place pensions. A PwC survey of 130 companies showed that 26 per cent of them are reviewing the role of pensions for all of their employees because of the changes to the annual allowance and the lifetime allowance for higher earners from April 2016.[10] Public sector workers are also demanding changes to their remuneration packages if they have already reached the new April 2016 lifetime allowance.

More again in 2017 with the secondary market in annuities

Throughout 2016, and from April 2017 onwards, we can expect to learn more about the secondary market in annuities – the sell back of annuities to insurance companies for cash. To help with consumer protection, consumers will, for example, have to take mandatory advice. The overall concern, however, is whether consumers will receive good value on the sale of their annuities, and initial views are that the new system is likely to be very complex.

Portal Financial Research has suggested that the buy-back terms are likely to 'very poor',[11] but the consumer may obtain slightly better value if the annuity is sold back to the insurance company which originally provided the annuity. There is some real value in the insurance company buying back its own annuities – like ending the expense of providing the annuity's income stream and the capital savings flowing from the cancellation of the annuity. However, this could also weaken the value of any newly purchased annuities and that market is already weakening.

According to research from Money Facts, annuity rates in 2015 fell for the second year running due to the introduction of the new pension freedoms, low gilt yields, and industry preparations for the new regulations.[12] Rates made a slight recovery over the summer of 2015, but then experienced sharp reductions during the final three months of 2015, with the average standard annuity rate falling by 3.24 per cent in the final quarter of 2015 (according to Retirement Advantage).[13] Perhaps it is not surprising that the FCA retirement income market data from July to September 2015 shows that, during that time, 178,999 pensions were accessed by individuals to take an income or fully withdraw their money as cash, rather than used to buy annuity.[14]

Although changes made recently by the European Insurance and Occupation Pensions Authority (EIOPA) to the new Solvency II regime will help prevent some further rises to annuity rates arising from that legislation, Solvency II is also having an impact on annuity rates according to Retirement Advantage, with the difference between the best and the worst open market annuity rates ranging from 11 and 17 per cent.[15]

So, have the pension reforms been a success?

Although it is still early days, taken as a whole, the changes appear to be good both for consumers and for generating consumer confidence. They have also successfully shaken up and forced a somewhat complacent pensions industry to re-invent itself and innovate. It remains debatable whether the next set of pension tax changes due for April 2016 will be so beneficial. The secondary market in annuities still has to evolve and have regulation set up before judgment can be passed as to whether it looks like it might be a success.

References

1. Resolution Foundation, 'Share of wealth owned by the recently retired has now overtaken the under 45s' (press release), 10 December 2015; available at: www.resolutionfoundation.org/media/press-releases/7735/.
2. FCA, 'Retirement Income Market Data', July–September 2015; available at: www.fca.org.uk/static/documents/retirement-income-market-data-july-september-2015.pdf.
3. Research from My Pension Expert, 10 December 2015; available at: www.mypensionexpert.com/news_wp/2015/12/shopping-around-annuity-net-extra.33-income-average-retirement/.

4. ONS, 'Statistical bulletin: MQ5: Investment by Insurance Companies, Pension Funds and Trusts, Quarter 3 (July to September) 2015'; available at: www.ons.gov.uk/ons/rel/fi/mq5--investment-by-insurance-companies--pension-funds-and-trusts/q3-2015/stb-mq5-q3-2015.html.
5. According to research from Portal Financial, as reported in: www.pensionsage.com/pa/Annuity-resale-returns-expected-to-be-very-poor.php.
6. MRM Young Money Report 2015, 'From Austerity to Aspiration'; available at: http://myfs-events.co.uk/wp-content/uploads/2015/12/Young-Money-Report-2015.pdf.
7. The Share Centre, 'One in ten holding out for an inheritance to fund their future'; available at: www.share.com/blog/2015/december/one-in-ten-holding-out-for-an-inheritance-to-fund-their-future/.
8. Xafinity, 'Number of DB transfers reaches new high for 2015 (media release); available at: www.xafinity.com/c_m_s/posts/sendfile/169.
9. RSM, 'Pension fraud risk report', 9 December 2015; available at www.rsmuk.com/ideas-and-insights/2015/dec/pensions-fraud-risk-report.
10. PwC, 'Pension tax changes are forcing companies to rethink higher earners' reward packagess', 23 December 2015; available at: http://pwc.blogs.com/press_room/2015/12/pension-tax-changes-are-forcing-companies-to-rethink-higher-earners-reward-packages.html.
11. As reported by Tuck, N., 'Annuity resale returns expected to be "very poor", *Pensions Age*, 17 December 2015; available at: www.pensionsage.com/pa/Annuity-resale-returns-expected-to-be-very-poor.php.
12. 'Another poor year for annuity rates', *Money Facts*, 11 January 2016; available at: https://moneyfacts.co.uk/news/annuities/another-poor-year-for-annuity-rates/.
13. Retirement Advantage, 'Solvency II highlights need to shop around', 11 January 2016; available at: http://newsroom.retirementadvantage.com/solvency-ii-highlights-need-to-shop-around/.
14. See note 2 above.
15. See note 13 above.

Chapter 10:
Paying for care – An update

By Lisa Morgan, partner at Hugh James

The issue of who pays for care continues to be a contentious topic. This article examines the current position of paying for care in England.

NHS funding

As a department, the Hugh James nursing care team continue to advise significantly on the issue of whether an individual should have been or should be in receipt of NHS continuing healthcare funding. The NHS is responsible for meeting the full cost of care home fees for individuals whose primary need for care is because of their health. This is known as NHS continuing healthcare (CHC) and is often described as 'fully funded care'. If an individual is found eligible for NHS CHC in a care home, they do not have to make any contribution to the cost of that care, regardless of the individual's means or the setting of their care.

However, despite the implementation of the National Framework ('the Framework') in October 2007 (updated July 2009 and revised in November 2012) and accompanying Decision Support Tool ('the Tool'), health authorities continue to make incorrect assessments of individuals' needs, leading to both significant financial charges being made and, moreover, individuals having to sell their family homes to pay for the cost of their care.

Further, despite the Framework being introduced with the hope of removing the 'postcode lottery' of eligibility, a clear disparity across England of who is eligible for NHS CHC sadly still remains. Statistics published by the Health and Social Care Information Centre on December 2015 confirm that, indeed, NHS continuing healthcare funding can vary dramatically depending on where you live. Examples include: NHS Aylesbury Vale who currently fund 12.41 people out of every 50,000 (as at September 2015), while NHS Salford funds 214.05 in every 50,000. NHS Croydon currently pays for 128.83, while NHS Wokingham now pays for 16.95 people, and NHS Blackpool for 86.63 in every 50,000.[1]

Unfortunately, these statistics only further highlight that there continues to be an inconsistent approach by health authorities in England to assessing NHS continuing healthcare, and the system remains unfair.

Retrospective reviews

Retrospectively, as a department, we have successfully recovered over £70 million in wrongly paid care home fees for our clients. However, there continues to be significant concerns about the delays in progressing retrospective reviews for NHS continuing healthcare. Since the Department of Health announced a close down of claims in England for wrongly paid care home fees for the period 1 April 2004 to 31 March 2011, it is estimated that health authorities have received in excess of 60,000 claims. Inevitably, this has caused significant delays in health authorities progressing reviews; many of our clients have now been waiting for over three years for their cases to be considered and are disappointed and feel let down by the system.

However, as a department, health authorities are beginning to inform us that the backlog of claims received as a result of the Department of Health's close down project will be considered by March 2017. While assessment timescales do vary depending on the health authority responsible for considering the case, generally, health authorities have started to make inroads into the backlog of claims. Additionally, many health authorities are outsourcing work to third parties in the hope that this will further expedite the completion of retrospective reviews. However, while the health authorities are beginning to reduce the number of claims received over recent months, there is a high level of doubt as to whether these claims will be considered and completed by March 2017.

As well as long delays, over the past few years we are also witnessing many claims where health authorities are refusing to undertake a retrospective review of an individual's needs when they were previously assessed for CHC funding. Many of our clients have waited over three years only to be informed by the health authority that their case is closed due to past assessments being completed, many of which our clients were neither aware of at the time nor were they informed of the outcome.

It became apparent, quite quickly, that health authorities were simply closing cases when it could be identified that past assessments had been undertaken on the individual. However, this should not be the case in light of guidance issued by the Department of Health in October 2012 entitled 'NHS Continuing Healthcare Review Process' ('the Guidance'). The Guidance and its content are discussed in context below.

As a result of the health authorities increasing trend to refuse reviews based on past CHC assessments, in one particular case, Bradford Clinical Commissioning Group (CCG) was criticised, by way of a judicial review application, in relation to their unlawful decision to refuse to undertake a retrospective review of CHC for part of the patient's period of care – *R (On the application of Neal Dennison Administrator of the Late Lily Dennison) v Bradford District Clinical Commissioning Group* [2014] EWHC 2552 ('*Dennison*').

Dennison: The facts

The claimant is the son of the late Lily Dennison ('LD') who was a resident in a nursing home in Bradford from January 2006 until she sadly passed away in October 2008. LD had to pay for the costs of her accommodation and non-nursing care costs as she had been assessed as not eligible for CHC during her time at the home. In September 2012, the claimant formally requested that LD's eligibility for CHC be reviewed retrospectively by the former Bradford and Airedale Primary Health Care Trust ('PCT').

The PCT agreed to assess LD's health and nursing needs during the period January 2006 and May 2007, but it refused to assess her health and nursing needs during the period May 2007 until October 2008. The PCT's refusal was on the basis that past assessments had been completed on LD in both May and September 2007 and then again in March 2008 that indicated she was not eligible for CHC.

The claimant sought judicial review of this decision on the basis that the assessments completed on LD were not clinically sound. Therefore, the PCT's decision to refuse to undertake a retrospective review of her needs was unreasonable in light of the Guidance.

Significantly, paragraph 4.1.6(i) of the Guidance states that if an individual has been previously assessed for CHC, the health authority should consider whether the past assessments were:

- Completed appropriately;
- Clinically sound;
- Reflected the patient information at the time; and
- Relate to the relevant period(s).

Additionally, paragraph 4.1.6(ii) of the Guidance confirms that if the individual was in receipt of either Registered Nursing Care Contributions (RNCC) or NHS Funded Nursing Care (FNC) (which LD was), these assessments should only have taken place when it had been established that the individual was not eligible for CHC.

In considering the claimant's application, the Honourable Mr Justice William Davis (Davis J) accepted that the assessments completed in May and September 2007 were both unreasonable and irrational. Davis J also recognised that in May 2007, the CHC checklist document was carried out after the RNCC determination. Therefore, a proper application of the standard practice at the time was not followed. Davis J confirmed that a proper application of paragraph 4.1.6(ii) of the Guidance by the PCT would have led to a review of the assessment in May 2007.

Similarly, Davis J also recognised that the PCT failed to follow their own local policy in respect of the September 2007 assessment through failing to complete a CHC assessment before completing a RNCC determination. Davis J did, however, submit that the assessment undertaken on LD in March 2008 was completed appropriately and the CCG's decision not to assess eligibility after this date was reasonable.

***Dennison*: Comment**

The outcome in *Dennison* certainly highlights the importance of CCG's applying the Guidance appropriately and, moreover, reinforces the conclusions of the court in *R (Grogan) v Bexley Health Trust* [2006] EWCA 44 that if an individual was in receipt of RNCC or FNC, the assessment for that funding should only take place once it has been established that the individual is not eligible for NHS CHC.

Further, *Dennison* confirms that while the remit of paragraph 4.1.6(ii) of the Guidance does not expressly state that if an RNCC assessment preceded the CHC assessment, a further assessment of a past period of care is necessary, the court was satisfied that it was implied in the terms of the paragraph. Davis J asserted that, 'were it to do otherwise, the PCT (or CCG) would be acting unlawfully'.

Therefore, in accordance with *Dennison*, health authorities should agree to undertake a review of any case whereby the individual was subject to RNCC or FNC assessments with no evidence of CHC having been considered, or when CHC was considered following RNCC or FNC.

***Dennison*: 17 months on**

Following *Dennison*, it was hoped that the judgment would have an implication on all cases where health authorities are refusing, unreasonably, to undertake a review of past assessments and, in particular, those cases whereby the individual was considered for RNCC/FNC before CHC was considered, or where is no evidence of CHC being considered at all.

However, while some health authorities will acknowledge the Guidance and the judgment in *Dennison* and agree to review previously assessed periods of care, many continue to ignore and misapply the Guidance and simply refuse to review the case when there is evidence of past assessments. The concerning factor is that, not only does a postcode lottery exist in terms of who is in receipt of CHC across England, but additionally in relation to how health authorities are dealing with claims relating to previously assessed periods of care. This only further evidences that the system remains unfair and that, significantly, many individuals who should have been in receipt of CHC funding are at risk of being overlooked.

Redress

On 1 April 2015, NHS England published its 'NHS Continuing Healthcare Refreshed Redress Guidance' ('the 2015 Guidance') which assists health authorities when settling claims for eligibility for CHC both currently and retrospectively. The aim of the 2015 Guidance was to refresh previous guidance ('NHS Continuing Healthcare: Continuing Care Redress') published by the Department of Health in March 2007 ('the 2007 Guidance').

Under the 2007 Guidance, an individual was entitled to request that interest on reimbursement of wrongly paid care home fees is calculated at both County Court Judgement (CCJ) and Retail Price Index (RPI) rate and entitled to the higher sum of two calculations.

However, under the 2015 Guidance, the health authority is no longer obliged to calculate interest using CCJ rate and the Guidance advises interest to be calculated using RPI rate only. Therefore, in accordance with the 2015 Guidance, an individual is now only entitled to interest at RPI rate on a decision resulting in restitution. This seems particularity unfair to those individuals who have been waiting for over three years for their cases to be considered by the health authority through no fault of their own.

The purpose of restitution is to put the individual back in the position they would have been in had the maladministration not occurred. While the calculation of interest should not lead to the claimant being unjustly enriched, it is debatable whether the removal of CCJ rate of interest is reasonable and fair.

For example, it is particularly unfair on those individuals who were not in receipt of any welfare benefits during the period of eligibility awarded. From experience, in these cases, the difference between RPI rate and CCG rate of interest, in financial terms, can be substantial; CCJ rate often produces a significantly higher rate of interest.

It can also be argued that reimbursement based on RPI rate is not always sufficient to put the individual back in the position they would have been in had the maladministration not occurred. In certain circumstances, individuals may have invested monies not used to pay for care and such investments would have produced a much greater yield than RPI rate interest does.

A further issue that has arisen as a result of the 2015 Guidance is that some health authorities are applying it to decisions in respect of eligibility that were made prior to its publication. This is incorrect. The 2015 Guidance clearly states that it shall only apply to decisions made on or after the date of publication (1 April 2015). Again, health authorities are sadly applying guidance inconsistently and some individuals are now finding themselves in a position where they are only given the option of RPI rate of interest despite the decision in respect of eligibility being made prior to the publication of the 2015 Guidance.

Local authorities charging for residential accommodation

When it is established that an individual is not the responsibility of the NHS, the local authority is under a duty to provide care and accommodation. Accommodation can be provided by a home managed by the local authority, or alternatively, in a privately owned care home. In either case, and from 1 April 2015, the Care Act 2014 (CA 2014) empowers the local authority, at their discretion, to charge the individual for both residential and non-residential services.

The local authority will complete a financial assessment to establish the extent to which they will be required to pay for their own residential fees. Currently, in England, if an individual's capital exceeds £23,250 they will be responsible, in full, for the cost their care. If the individual holds capital of £14,250 but less than £23,250, they will be treated as having a tariff income and will be required to pay an additional £1 per week for every £250 of capital they hold. If an individual's capital exceeds the upper limit, the local authority is prohibited from contributing to the fees.

The Care and Support (Charging and Assessment of Resources) Regulations 2014 ('the Charging Regulations') replace the Charging for Residential Accommodation Guide (CRAG). The Charging Regulations largely replicate CRAG with the exception of some new elements.

Significantly, the Regulations reflect and confirm the 2:1 majority decision in *Walford v Worcestershire County Council*.[2] Schedule 2, paragraph 4 of the Charging Regulations now make clear that a 'qualifying relative' must have occupied their main or only home before the individual was first accommodated in a care home under the CA 2014 to qualify for the mandatory disregard.

This will be disappointing for many who considered the judgment in *Walford*, at first instance, to be a victory for all families of individuals in care who wish to protect the family home from the local authority.

The cap on care costs

The 'cap on care costs' has been widely reported since the CA 2014 received Royal Assent on 14 May 2014. Section 15 of the

CA 2014 allows for regulations to establish the amount that individuals can be required to pay towards the cost of care during their lifetime. The cap will prevent local authorities from making a charge for meeting needs (other than for daily living costs[3]) once the individual's personal lifetime cap has been reached. The personal cap has been proposed at a level of £72,000.

However, whether care is provided in your home or in a residential home, only the rate set by the local authority will count towards the cap of £72,000.[4] Therefore, in reality, individuals will pay more than £72,000 towards the cost of their care before the local authority becomes responsible.

The provisions in section 15 were due to be implemented on 1 April 2016, but the government has announced that the implementation of the personal lifetime cap will be delayed until April 2020. Amid concerns that the cap would cost £6 billion over the next five years, in his written statement to parliament, Alistair Burt, minister of state for community and social care, stated: 'a time of consolidation is not the right moment to be implementing expensive new commitments such as this'.[5]

With average composite (state-funded, top-up, and pure pay combined) residential fees costing £563 per week and nursing fees at £756 per week,[6] the four-year delay will prove to be bitterly disappointing to those already in receipt of care. Paul Burstow, former Liberal Democrat care minister, stated: 'the decision to delay the cap will leave thousands of families facing catastrophic care'.[7]

While the government states that it continues to be 'firmly committed' to implementing the cap, others are not so sure and question whether the cap will be introduced at all. Richard Humphries, assistant director of The King's Fund, said that the reforms have been 'abandoned, not postponed'.[7]

Deferred payment agreements

Prior to the implementation of the CA 2014, deferred payment agreements (DPA) were offered at the discretion of the local authority. This has now been extended and reformed by the CA 2014 and local authorities are now obliged, in defined circumstances, to enter into DPAs. DPAs assist individuals in ensuring that they are not forced to sell their homes to pay for the cost of their care. The council will allow the individual to take out a loan that is secured against their property. The loan will be repaid upon the sale of the home.

While the CA 2014 has made DPAs more widely available to individuals across England, the CA 2014 allows local authorities to charge interest on their loans as well an arrangement fee. Interest is expected to be charged at 2.65 per cent.[9]

References

1. Health & Social Care Information Centre, 'NHS Continuing Healthcare Activity Statistics for England, Quarter 2 2015-16 Report, Experimental Statistics', December 2015; available at: www.hscic.gov.uk/catalogue/PUB19312.
2. *Walford v Worcestershire County Council* [2015] EWCA Civ 22.
3. Even when the cap is reached, individuals living in care homes will still be responsible for meeting the cost of their food and lodging. It has been reported that a flat rate of £230 a week has been proposed.
4. For example, if the local authority is willing to pay £450 a week for care, for individuals falling within that local authority's responsibility, the £72,000 cap on care costs will not be reached until 160 weeks of care have been paid for.
5. In a letter to the chair of the Local Government Association; letter available at: www.gov.uk/government/uploads/system/uploads/attachment_data/file/446309/Cap_on_care_acc.pdf.
6. Laing Buisson, Press Release, 30 September, 2015; available at: www.laingbuisson.co.uk/MediaCentre/PressReleases/CareofOlderPeople27th.aspx.
7. As reported in the *Telegraph* on 17 July 2015; see: www.telegraph.co.uk/news/health/elder/11746216/Tories-poised-to-delay-flagship-cap-on-care-costs.html.
8. Humphries, R., 'Paying for care: back to square one?'; available at: www.kingsfund.org.uk/blog/2015/07/paying-care-back-square-one.
9. As reported by the BBC on 22 July 2015; see: www.bbc.co.uk/news/health-30922484.

Chapter 11:
Active and passive investment strategies – Weighing up the options

By Claire Bennison, regional director at Brooks Macdonald Asset Management

Investors have long debated the relative merits of active and passive investment strategies. In summary, active investment involves utilising the knowledge, skill, and experience of a fund manager to try to achieve better returns than a benchmark (alpha). Conversely, passive investment generally involves using a tracking strategy to mirror the performance of a particular index (beta). The latter can be achieved through ownership of an exchange-traded fund (ETF) or an index fund.

Efficient markets theory

Arguably, whether an investor will favour an active or passive approach will depend on their view of the Efficient Market Hypothesis. The hypothesis, the work of Eugene Fama,[1] came to the forefront of academic studies on investment returns in the 1970s. At this time, Fama presented an argument that an efficient market is one where all publicly available and relevant past information is incorporated in market prices and that all new information is immediately discounted. For investors that believe this is true, the assumption is that it would be difficult to generate better returns than the benchmark and a passive investment approach is most efficient.

The market capitalisation approach

Since the 1970s we have seen increased growth in vehicles that offer passive means of tracking index returns, with the first market-capitalisation weighted passive equity index created in 1973. Since then, this sector of the market has grown and according to the Investment Association (IA) Annual Survey of the UK Fund Management Industry, 20 per cent of UK assets under management are managed on a 'fully passive basis'.[2]

The indices against which passive investment strategies are managed are largely established on a market-capitalised basis (a company's market capitalisation is calculated by multiplying the number of shares it has issued by its share price). Historically, indices have favoured the capitalisation-based weighting methodology as it is deemed to reflect both the reality of a company's economic size and the subjective market opinion of the company through its share price.

A major challenge to this type of construction is that it over-weights overvalued stocks and under-weights undervalued stocks. This can lead to large distortions for individual stocks or assets, both positively and negatively, exposing investors to high concentration risk should asset bubbles form. One example of this was Cisco at the height of the 'DotCom Bubble'; from 1999 to 2000, Cisco's market-capitalised weighting rose from 1.7 per cent to a staggering 4.1 per cent as exuberance took hold of the stock market.

A passive investment vehicle can be constructed in various forms. The simplest strategy is 'full replication' where vehicles are created with stocks held at the same proportionate weight as they are represented within the relevant benchmark index. A more complex passive strategy is 'optimisation' where if, for example, not all stocks within the index can be held, the difference between a passive vehicle and the index is minimised. Other forms include 'synthetic' vehicles, where derivative products are used; or a 'blend', which is a mix between full replication and optimisation. An index fund is similar to an ETF in that it is a collective investment fund, but is subject to daily pricing rather than intra-day pricing.

Low-cost beta and transparency

What passive investment strategies did engender was a defined 'rules-based' approach to the portfolio construction process that provides transparency. For example, for such a strategy, investors know that:

1. At the end of the period all stocks in the index upon which the passive investment strategy is based, for example the London Stock Exchange, will be reviewed;
2. The review will identify specific stocks by market capitalisation;
3. These stocks will then be included or removed at a specific time; and
4. The strategy will then hold these stocks until the next review period and the process will then be repeated.

Proponents of passive investing cite a number of other benefits, over and above the difficulty in outperforming a benchmark index. One of the most commonly presented arguments is the low-cost compared to active fund management fees. In addition, given the size of this sector, liquidity concerns are reduced (particularly in the key developed markets).

Understanding active management

However, not all investors believe that the Efficient Market Hypothesis perfectly describes markets in practice. Investment Association data would suggest 80 per cent of investors still favour active management, primarily through collective investment schemes.

Active management strategies seek to use the knowledge, skill, and experience of a fund manager to achieve alpha, or the return achieved above that of the market, i.e. beta. In a basic passive strategy, gross of fees, you would expect to see zero alpha; while an active manager, gross of fees, is looking to achieve a positive alpha (a return in excess of the market).

To do this, they will employ various processes such as quantitative reviews of companies based on different factors (such as price to earnings or free cash flow). Furthermore, they may analyse company accounts and meet company management to identify the value of the company and compute the expected return of the company against that of its peer group and market. They can incorporate views of sectors they favour based on their macroeconomic view, they can overlay their outlook with technical and momentum indicators. The number of different ways of achieving alpha through an active approach is long.

Each active fund manager will have a mandate they need to keep to and when investment analysts review the fund manager's returns their due diligence focuses not only on the investment performance, but also on the investment risk taken to achieve it, the liquidity of the fund, and its cost.

Comparing returns

Generally, each fund has an idea of what its turnover (buying and selling of securities) is likely to be. One of the primary arguments favouring passive over active strategies is the fact that they can operate on lower costs. Historically, this has been true and it is still generally true today, but the gap in pricing between active and passive funds is reducing – especially as institutional managers can now benefit from clean share classes where fees are reduced. This suggests that active fund fees' higher drag on net returns is likely to diminish further over time.

Beyond cost, the debate over whether active or passive strategies are more attractive is likely to continue to rumble on ad infinitum. What experience has demonstrated is that in certain market cycles either passive or active solutions can perform better. There is an argument that suggests that when a market is in the first stage of a 'bull' market and all stocks go up regardless of the fundamentals a passive approach may

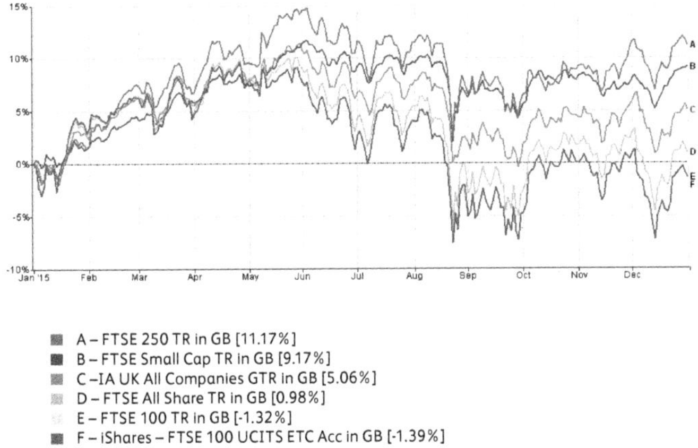

Figure 1: Comparison performance of UK markets, 1 January to 31 December 2015. Source: Financial Express

make more sense. That said, there are cycles where the ability of active management to limit exposure to sectors or stocks that are likely to underperform will be beneficial.

In the past year, when considering the active and passive debate, commentators have focused attention on the performance of the UK. Figure 1 provides the return of a number of FTSE indices compared against one of the more popular passive vehicles that investors use to gain UK equity exposure, the iShares FTSE 100 Exchange Traded Fund (ETF) (which aims to track the performance of the FTSE 100 index as closely as possible), and the IA UK All Companies Index, which can be considered as a representation of active UK equity managers (although we would note over 10 per cent of this index is also comprised of tracker investments).

Figure 1 demonstrates that the active IA UK All Companies gained +5.06 per cent compared to the iShare FTSE 100 ETF loss of -1.39 per cent during the past year, suggesting that active managers, gross of fees, have outperformed passive managers (the drag that turnover can have is also seen from the FTSE 100 return compared to the iShare, with the iShare marginally underperforming the index by 0.07 per cent). This can be attributed to the fact that the FTSE 100 has struggled in the past year due to its high weighting towards the energy and mining sectors, which active managers have largely avoided. Commodity-based securities have suffered amid concerns regarding China's economic slowdown, while the energy sector has declined alongside the sharp fall in oil prices over the past year (Brent crude fell by 44.1 per cent in 2015).

Viewed from a FTSE 100 perspective, active management seems to have been beneficial. However, this is not true when you examine some of the other main indices in the UK. The mid-cap FTSE 250 and the FTSE Small Cap index have both outperformed the active proxy index of the UK All Companies. This suggests that, at the very least, it is important to have an active management overlay of investments, such as an active decision on asset allocation to identify the sectors that are likely to outperform in a particular cycle.

So, is this assessment true over other time periods? If we review the same benchmarks then the performances are not dissimilar. What is demonstrated again is that with turnover drag the iShare underperforms the FTSE 100 index it mirrors in each of the one, three, and five-year time periods, with the loss increasing to 1.73 per cent by year 5. If you consider what is arguably a more like-for-like comparison, assuming the FTSE All Share Total Return Index in GBP to be a passive proxy against an active proxy of the IA UK All Companies, then again in each time period we can see that the active approach outperforms the index, gross of fees, by: one year: 4.08 per cent; three year 10.52 per cent; five year 9.98 per cent. Even if costs were taken into account, this positive variance for active management would arguably still be in place.

Index	1 year (%)	3 year (%)	5 year (%)
FTSE 100 TR in GB	-1.32	17.96	26.89
FTSE 250 TR in GB	11.17	52.43	72.89
FTSE All Share TR in GB	0.98	23.43	33.82
FTSE Small Cap TR in GB	9.17	46.23	63.49
IA UK All Companies GTR in GB	5.06	33.95	43.80
iShares FTSE 100 ETF in GB	-1.39	17.31	25.16

Table 1: Performance of UK Markets: One, three, and five years until 31 December 2015. Source: Financial Express

Bridging the gap

The debate surrounding active and passive investment strategies has moved on in recent years, particularly given the growing popularity of 'smart beta' products, which arguably bridge the gap between passive and active investment strategies. The name 'smart beta' lacks a strict definition, but it can be used to describe any of a number of investment strategies. Products such as 'strategic beta', 'alternative beta', 'enhanced beta', or 'advanced beta' all fall under the smart beta moniker, although they are all essentially passive funds taking active positions that are determined using pre-defined rules.

At a basic level, smart beta strategies are designed to add value by systematically selecting, weighting, and rebalancing a portfolio's individual investments based on characteristics other than market capitalisation. For example, fundamental smart beta strategies select and weight investments based on characteristics such as dividends, book value, and cash flow metrics.

The variety of such products has been increasing for some time and, nowadays, products targeting characteristics such as lower variance, increased diversification, and reduced volatility, as well as those that seek to benefit from market characteristics such as momentum, are widespread. Nevertheless, they all share similar goals – to generate alpha, lower risk, or increase diversification in a cost-efficient manner.

Accessing smart beta products

One of the key challenges of smart beta strategies is understanding how to use them. As they are relatively new to the market place (the oldest smart beta funds are only 10 years old), directly assessing how they are likely to perform against specific economic and financial backdrops is somewhat problematic. Instead, investors must use their expertise to assess whether the underlying methodologies underpinning the products are appropriate. However, this can be difficult as some products, such as those targeting reduced volatility, break away from the views of traditional modern portfolio theory (in this case, investors need to take higher risk in order to gain the potential for higher returns).

Despite the fact that such strategies may ignore tried-and-tested traditional portfolio theory, some investors seem to be convinced. In the year to 30 September 2015, global smart beta products accounted for 30 per cent of asset flows into 'passive' exchange-traded products. This is because back-testing of such strategies provides compelling results; analysed over the period between 1963 and 2014, a portfolio investing in the 10 per cent of US stocks with the lowest historic volatility would have produced an annualised return of 10.7 per cent, while a portfolio consisting of the 10 per cent of stocks with the highest volatility would have returned only 4.6 per cent per year.[3] It is worth noting that there is no such thing as a bad successful back-test on a product coming to market.

However, improved returns are not the only driver of investor interest. Surveyed evidence suggests that other key benefits include improvements in diversification and risk reduction.[4] Costs are another factor that could be expected to be driving demand for such assets, particularly given their classification as 'passive' products; however, the expense ratios of smart beta strategies range significantly (roughly from 0.6 per cent to 2.3 per cent per annum) and do not necessarily provide an advantage over their active counterparts.

For the moment, smart beta strategies are largely focused towards equities, rather than bonds (although this is starting to change with new bond products coming to the fore), with investors seemingly favouring strategies that target low volatility, those that seek to generate outperformance by analysing dividend characteristics, and those that employ multi-factor methodologies (i.e. those that seek to weight constituents by an assessed intrinsic value, rather than by market capitalisation).[5]

Constructing investment portfolios

It is clear that investors have judged smart beta products as having at least some success in breaking the link between market-capitalisation weighted passive strategies and their active counterparts. However, market cycles will continue to dictate returns and having the flexibility and knowledge to know when to utilise which assets will remain key to the success of any overarching asset allocation strategy.

Increased choice provides further opportunity for diversification and the advent of these products provides further scope for investors to generate added value. However, as with all investments, investors must be careful to undertake the necessary due diligence to ensure that they understand the products they are utilising and what exposure they are adding to portfolios. Likewise, they must account for their cost and liquidity characteristics.

Given increased choice, new products, and evolution of markets, a number of professional advisers and clients now choose to outsource their investment management to a discretionary fund manager, who is able to use their specific expertise to make active asset allocation decisions and construct investment portfolios with both active and passive strategies.

References

1. Fama, E., 'Efficient Capital Markets: A Review of Theory and Empirical Work', *Journal of Finance* 25 (2): 383-417, 1970.
2. Clare, A. Prof, 'Smart Beta: Part One: Origins', Powershares by Invesco, 2015; available at: www.cassknowledge.com/sites/default/files/article-attachments/what-is-smart-beta-cass-business-school-invesco-powershares-part-1-nov-2015.pdf.
3. Ibid.
4. Spence J., 'Unconstrained fixed income: Providing yields and rate risk protection', *Deeper Perspectives*, Number 29, July 2015; available at: www.spencejohnson.com/research/download/126.
5. 'Smart Beta Trends & Flows', Morningstar Direct – Powershares by Invesco, 30 September 2015.

Chapter 12: How legal and financial advisers can work together more effectively

By Ian Muirhead, chairman of SIFA

Few solicitors have seriously got to grips with financial services work. During the 1990s, when the Law Society was responsible for regulation and supported solicitors' involvement in financial services through a dedicated working party, 235 firms established an in-house financial services department. However, after 2001 when the Financial Services Authority (FSA) became the sole regulator, many of these firms threw in the towel, and there are now barely more than 20 law firms in England and Wales which are jointly regulated by the Solicitors Regulation Authority (SRA) and the FSA's successor, the Financial Conduct Authority (FCA), and which provide retail financial services to their clients.

There are a number of reasons for this retreat. First, in the same way as solicitors dipped a toe into the estate agency market in the 1980s, many assumed that if they appointed what appeared to be a competent manager, they could delegate responsibility and forget. In the case of both estate agency and financial services, they failed to appreciate the complementary nature of the two activities and to involve themselves sufficiently to understand how their new business worked. To an extent this was due to a feeling of professional superiority over non-solicitors, but it also underlined solicitors' limitations as business managers – particularly when the additional activity is non-mainstream. Solicitors' heightened awareness of risk and their propensity to see the problem in every solution equips them poorly for entrepreneurial enterprise.

Another factor in the fall-out which followed 2001 was the abrasive style of the FSA. Its mission was to cleanse the Augean stables and put an end to the poor quality of financial advice which had resulted from the profit fixation and from the limited training of the salespeople who had been drafted into the service of the life companies after becoming unemployed during the Thatcher regime of the 1980s. The idea of a regulator which named and shamed and fined was alien to solicitors whose concept of regulation had always been founded in ethics. The fact that this change in regulation happened at a time when stock markets were reeling from the tech bust, with the result that income was going down at the same time as costs were going up, provided further discouragement to staying in the game.

The way we are now

The picture has now changed dramatically, and there is widespread evidence of solicitors seeking links of whatever sort with financial advisers. This reflects a number of factors. First, an awareness of the fact that the FSA made very substantial strides in improving standards of financial advice. Commission, the great sales motivator, has now been banned except in relation to protection business, and a new minimum standard qualification level of QCF4 has been established. Indeed, many top-end advisers have now gone further and acquired chartered status.

The second factor is an increasing recognition among solicitors of the synergy between legal and financial work, particularly in relation to matrimonial matters, older clients, trusts, and estate planning. The most significant development in this area has been George Osborne's 'pension freedoms', as a result of which pensions have become the prime estate planning tool. Until 6 April 2015, the value of a personal pension or other defined contribution pension plan was subject to a 55 per cent 'death tax' on the death of the plan holder; and bearing in mind that pensions are usually people's second biggest asset, after their house, the knowledge that a substantial part of the benefit of the plan would go to the taxman rather than the deceased's beneficiaries was a major discouragement to pension saving.

Now, if the plan holder dies before reaching the age of 75, the full value of the plan can be passed to anyone of the plan holder's choosing, including a trust, in the form of tax-free income. On death after the age of 75, the person receiving the benefit is taxable on its value at the rate of 45 per cent until 5 April 2016 and thereafter at the recipient's own rate of income tax. As the rules currently stand, this can apply from one generation to another. No inheritance tax is payable and the recipient only pays income tax when drawing income from what continues to be essentially a tax-free fund.

Beneficiaries must be identified in a form of nomination, which must be provided to the administrators of the scheme, and it is important that this should be reviewed regularly and kept up-to-date as family circumstances change. In addition, it is usually desirable for a fuller account of the plan holder's intentions to be provided to their trustees in the form of a 'letter of wishes'.

As a result of these additional benefits of pensions, it is now commonly accepted that as far as retirement income is concerned, it makes sense to exhaust all other sources of income before tapping into the pension fund.

The third major reason for solicitors' re-awakened interest in financial services is, of course, the impact of the Legal Services Act on solicitors' traditional business preserve. The overriding objective of the Act is to increase access to legal advice by permitting lawyers other than solicitors and barristers to enter into the market, but what is significant is that whereas the new entrants are regarding the Act as providing the opportunity to diversify their business proposition by adding legal services to their portfolio, solicitors are for the most part sticking to their traditional business model and limiting themselves to bringing non-lawyers onto their management teams. Very few are embracing the multi-disciplinary business model, although many are strengthening their ties with third party financial advisers.

This cautious approach is probably prudent, bearing in mind that most solicitors' firms are not sufficiently well organised internally to enable them to participate meaningfully in a third party corporate relationship. The 'confederation of sole practitioners' syndrome still persists in many firms, and far too many managing partners still plead, 'I couldn't possibly tell my partners what to do!'

Outcomes-focused regulation (OFR)

A major issue here lies in the fact that the profession as a whole has failed to understand the system of OFR. This was thrust upon the SRA by the Legal Services Board, on the basis that it worked in 2001 when seven financial services regulators were replaced by a single regulator, the FSA, and that it should in theory also work in a situation where there are now 11 front-line legal regulators overseeing a wide variety of business models. In theory, the application of the system should revolve around the compliance officer, but many law firm compliance officers do not fully understand their role and the SRA has even proposed – ludicrously – that smaller firms should be exempted from the requirement to appoint compliance officers.

The reason why OFR (aka principles-based) regulation worked in the financial services sector was because the FSA made as its over-arching requirement the need for the firms which it regulated to adopt formal management systems and controls, on the basis that if the management of a firm is running a tight ship, then to a large extent the rules will look after themselves. Principle 8 and Chapter 7 of the SRA Code of Conduct reflect these requirements, but the SRA has done nothing to enforce them, and the situation is exacerbated by the disconnect which exists between the regulatory role of the SRA and the support and guidance role of the Law Society. Lexcel, which has the potential to fill this role, fails even to address the roles of COLP and COFA and remains pre-occupied with traditional and ethical issues.

A particular issue in relation to OFR arises in the context of 'compulsory professional development' (CPD). Under the FCA regime, the identification of the need for training, the learning outcomes sought from CPD, the identification and approval of appropriate sources and types of training, the analysis of the effectiveness of training which has been completed, the possible need for gap-filling, the impact of training decisions on plans for other members of the firm, and the selection of training organisations, are all part of the regime which revolves around the establishment of HR procedures for job appraisals, personal development plans and key performance indicators. These basic elements of a structure for management systems and controls are as yet missing both from the SRA Code and the Lexcel support services, and one cannot help wondering how outcomes-focused CPD would be able to work in their absence.

Equally, complaints handling is much more rigorously enforced for financial advisers than for solicitors. The FCA's objective is to ensure that the reason for a complaint is addressed so that there will be no recurrence. The regulator asks what was the reason for the complaint? Was it a reflection on the firm's training and CPD requirements or was it due to a shortcoming on the part of an individual? In the former case, what has been done to improve the systems; and in the latter case, has that person's role been re-assessed or has remedial or disciplinary action been taken? And in both cases, where is the compliance audit trail?

Competition

Competition in the legal sector is highlighting solicitors' vulnerabilities, in particular their over-dependence on transactions, the absence of comprehensive client fact-finding, and the consequent absence of firm-wide client databases. Also, poor management standards. In a damning indictment of its own membership, the introduction to the Law Society's Financial Stability Toolkit, 2015 reported that 'The SRA's report on financial stability said its engagement with firms found poor financial management that ranged from naïve to reckless'.

Meanwhile, SRA director Crispin Passmore is demonstrating a reassuring awareness of the direction of travel for the professional services market. He commented in October 2014: 'We believe that these changes [arising from the Legal Services Act] will benefit consumers by providing greater competition in the provision of legal services, greater opportunities to access holistic services'. He envisages 'a market no longer defined by professional titles and one in which the artificial barriers created by those titles are breaking down rapidly'.

Aside from the very small list of reserved activities, all solicitors' work is up for grabs, not only from other authorised lawyers but also the providers of unregulated legal activities whose numbers are predicted by the LSB to eclipse the regulated sector. And, in this brave new world, clients – and indeed the courts – will expect solicitors to look outside the legal silo and address their clients' wider needs. Hence the class actions by aggrieved female divorce clients who have contended that their solicitors have failed to address the three options for pensions on divorce; and the right to buy clients who have complained that their solicitors neglected to address the incidental issues of finance and insurance. Indeed, due no doubt to the restricted public perception of solicitors' services and their arguably fusty image, some prominent firms of solicitors prefer to describe themselves as 'lawyers' and 'law firm' instead.

In this multi-disciplinary world, success will go to those whose business is relationship-based – which most law firms' model is not. Accountants have this and will soon be a major force in the probate market, the prediction being that 750 accountancy firms will satisfy the very nominal qualification requirement of attending a two-day course and obtaining a 50 per cent pass mark in multiple choice and short answer questions. Financial advisers also have the benefit of a relationship-based business, and the FCA requires that clients' changing circumstances should be kept under regular review.

But not only do solicitors lack this advantage. Most also lack the entrepreneurial instinct which might enable then to turn threat into opportunity. They prefer to remain within the comfort zone of the legal silo and to confine their development plans to mergers and consolidation, plugging gaps left by reduced personal injury and legal aid work from within the repertoire of traditional legal services. It is likely, therefore, that the stimulus for diversification will come from outside the profession.

To an extent, this may come from the accountants who are being recruited by some law firms as chief executives. But it may also come from professionals from other disciplines tacking legal services onto their existing business proposition. The Legal Ombudsman has astutely observed three logical areas of diversification: 'Professional services are increasingly being bundled together and there are overlaps between for example legal, financial, property and claims management companies'.

ABS and joint ventures

Legal-plus-financial ABSs are few and far between, one inhibiting factor being the SRA's concern that financial services claims should not wind up at the door of the Solicitors' Compensation Fund. For this reason, most of the existing examples have retained the regulatory autonomy of the legal and financial services units, but have wedded the two together with common management and shareholding and the secondment of staff between the two units, to ensure that each understands the other's role. However, the core of the business has been the IFA's FSA-ordained management systems and controls, its client database, the potential for cross-selling, and the greater marketability of financial services.

An early example of an alternative business structure (ABS) involving financial and legal services is Chesterton House, an IFA firm in the Midlands which has for many years operated a joint venture (JV) with a local law firm and now has an ABS in addition to this. The ABS is staffed by three solicitors, two of whom have STEP (Society of Trust and Estate Practitioner) qualifications and conduct wills, trusts, probate, property, and inter-generational family office activities, all of which have a clear financial services dimension. This is a prime example of the holistic business service envisaged by Crispin Passmore at the SRA. But it is managed by IFAs.

While the number of legal-plus-financial ABSs is small, there is widespread interest in JVs. Typically, these will take the form of a limited company which is jointly owned by the solicitors and the financial advisers and which, for regulatory purposes, is an 'appointed representative' of the IFA firm. This means that it is the IFA firm which is responsible to the FCA for compliance. The IFA firm will make all of its resources available to the JV and will levy a management charge to recover its costs. The dividend payable to the two sets of shareholders will be based on the net income.

Firms tend to gravitate to JV having first established arrangements for arms-length referrals, and the JV has the advantage that referrals can be remunerated by dividend. From the IFA's point of view, the JV creates a relationship between firms, as opposed to individuals, and therefore provides the basis for joint business planning. Questions which should be addressed include:

- What is the scope of the JV's expertise?
- Should arrangements be made with other IFAs to fill any gaps in the JV's expertise?
- Who will co-ordinate the law firm's involvement?
- Which legal services will require financial advice?
- Which fee-earners will be involved?
- Should staff be incentivised to refer cases?
- What are the likely numbers of cases?

- What should the minimum investment values be?
- What are the target income levels? and
- How regularly will performance be reviewed against budget?

The problem with JVs, and the reason that many fail to gain traction, is that it often proves impossible to get all the partners to commit to the success of the JV. Some harbour unnecessary doubts as to the legitimacy of dividend payments. Some want to maintain their personal IFA connections. Others feel that a JV relationship might compromise their independence, and tend to overlook the fact that the IFA partner firm should have been selected on the basis that its attributes distinguish it from possible alternatives as being most likely to be able to serve clients' best interests. This should provide reassurance even to deputies of the Court of Protection and trustees of controlled trusts.

Here again, the underlying problem is the lack of management disciplines within the law firm. Every referral of clients for financial advice should now comply with the requirement of Outcome 6.3 of the SRA Code of Conduct, that the referring solicitor or fee-earner should ensure that the client is satisfied that the referral will be in their best interest. This clearly implies that the referrer must first be satisfied that this is the case, and demands that the referrer should conduct due diligence on the referee. But it would be impracticable for every fee-earner to conduct their own due diligence, and best practice requires that decisions of this sort should be undertaken centrally by firms' managements, under the guidance of the compliance officer for legal practice, so as to avoid the risks which would arise if individual members of the firm were to take their own decisions, without any overall quality control.

Insofar as referrals to JVs are concerned, there is an additional requirement that clients must give their informed consent to referrals, though the LSB has specifically stated that the SRA will not interpret this requirement prescriptively; that is to say, that consent need not necessarily be confirmed in writing. Nevertheless, written consent is desirable if the SRA's concern is to be addressed that clients should be made aware that advice received from the JV will not have the benefit of the client protections afforded by the Solicitors' Compensation Fund and the Legal Ombudsman.

JVs have received a fillip from the SRA decision to permit solicitors' separate businesses (of which JVs are an example) to conduct non-reserved legal activities. This would permit a law firm to segment its business by, for example, routing its low-quality wills business through a JV so that it benefited from the absence of regulatory overheads. Currently, solicitors would not be permitted themselves to provide unregulated services through a separate business, but consideration is being given to the removal of even this restriction.

JVs are likely to suit smaller firms of similar size or individual departments within larger firms. IFAs with specialist business competencies beyond the norm would be more likely to wish to maintain relationships with a wider population of law firms. This is not to say that having a JV relationship would be likely to inhibit relations with other firms. On the contrary, there are many examples of firms with several JVs, often focused on a particular specialist business competence, such as personal injury work.

Client referrals

Although the number of JVs continues to grow, arms-length third party client referrals to IFAs remain the principal form of interaction between legal and financial advisers. Such referrals cannot feasibly be remunerated financially, but this does not preclude payment for legitimate marketing services. For example, if a law firm were to agree to make available to its clients the generic marketing and technical material of an IFA firm, to put a link on its website, and to participate in joint client seminars, then subject to the necessary disclosures and to a satisfactory compliance audit trail, this would be permitted and would indeed achieve many of the objectives of a JV. It would, however, be important to ensure that the marketing fee should not appear to amount to a commission related to individual financial transactions. The SRA would be likely to object if it took the view that the relationship amounted to a device for the remuneration of referrals.

Solicitors' overriding concern when working with financial advisers is that their clients should be in safe hands. The prohibition against referrals to what were previously known as 'tied agents' and now as 'restricted advisers' has now been abandoned, to the dismay of the Law Society, but solicitors should hopefully find it difficult to justify to clients the high charges, poor investment performance, and product lock-ins which characterise the business propositions of some national firms of restricted advisers.

The first item on any due diligence checklist should be the independence of the advisers, and qualifications should figure prominently. In this respect, the status of chartered or certified financial planner should be noted, as also should the accreditations awarded by the STEP and Resolution. Members of The Society of Later Life Advisers (SOLLA) also command respect. The way in which qualifications, accreditations, and business specialisations complement those of the law firm should also be emphasised in explaining the benefits of holistic advice; and in this respect clients are likely to be better served by IFAs than by a stockbroker or discretionary fund manager service which is confined to investment.

Conclusion

Prior to the Legal Services Act, solicitors had no need to think outside the legal silo, but now all and sundry competitors can provide legal services, whether regulated or unregulated, and they are combining these with complementary services which provide the basis for ongoing client relationships. Solicitors need to remain competitive in this new integrated market for professional services, and financial advisers have much to offer as business partners. However, the combination of disciples will only work effectively if solicitors can first learn to manage their own businesses, working as unified business units, with common practices, common objectives, shared client information, and adherence to common management disciplines. Management is the key to success, and a prime objective of law firm management should be to reduce dependence on transactional business by diversifying their client proposition.